HOW TO START A KINGDOM CONVERSATION

Sharing Christ with those Closest to You

By
Dr. Alfred L. "Duke" Heller, D.D.S., M.S.

BMH BOOKS
Winona Lake, Indiana
www.bmhbooks.com
2005

Scripture quotations, unless otherwise indicated, are from the New American Standard Bible®, Copyright © 1960, 1962, 1963, 1968, 1971, 1972, 1973, 1975, 1977, 1995 by The Lockman Foundation. Used by permission. www.Lockman.org

Scripture quotations marked KJV are from the Holy Bible, King James Version, 1611.

Cover design by Terry Julien
Internal page design and typesetting by Jim Folsom
Photos in chapter 6 by Kim Laurell

ISBN: 0-88469-082-2
Printed in the United States of America

BMH Books
P.O. Box 544
Winona Lake, IN 46590
www.bmhbooks.com

Dedication

I am in full time ministry; I just happen to do it as a dentist.

To my wife, Wanda, who has allowed me to live my dreams.
She has allowed me to excel in dentistry as well as live with my
passion to share Jesus Christ, often on very short notice, resulting in
her having to alter her plans.

I love you, Wanda!

And to Pastor John Willett,
who got me started in sharing my faith by
drawing on napkins in restaurants.
He discipled me for more than seven years by meeting with me
every Wednesday morning for one and a half hours
to help me better understand the Bible.
I love this man for what he does in sharing
the good news of the gospel.

Acknowledgements

I would like to acknowledge the help of Marlene Bagnull, my first editor who read the rough draft and helped me to organize the content. I would also like to thank Viki Rife for her help as an editor preparing the final drafts and helping with titles. Bill Palmateer helped with the design of the *Mayishare* brochure, and Mike Seemuller helped in the production of the video that can be used with the brochure.

I'm grateful for the work of Jesse Deloe and Terry White at BMH Books. Both have been extremely helpful in getting my message in print so the reader could relate better to the material.

Thanks also to Pastor Dick Mayhue who mentored me while running around a track memorizing the book of James. I especially want to thank Dr. Jim Custer, my pastor whose sermon was responsible for my accepting Christ, who has mentored me, counseled me, and loved me when he did not have to. I thank him, also, for his encouragement in producing a manuscript that could truly help people overcome their fear of sharing their faith.

— Duke Heller
March 2005

The poem in chapter five is used with permission of the author, Teresa "Wolfpoet" Piercy-Gates.

Material in chapter eight is taken from Ray Comfort: *Hell's Best Kept Secret.* New Kensington, PA: Whitaker House. Used with permission of the author.

Material in chapter eleven is taken from updates and reports of The Barna Group, Ventura, CA, and is used with permission. www.barna.org

Contents

Forewords

"Read With Joy and Commitment"
– Zig Ziglar

I believe there is a critical need within the Christian community for this book. *How to Start a Kingdom Conversation* is the heartfelt work of a man who knows and loves Christ and wants to share His grace, glory, love, and promises with others.

In this book my friend, Dr. Duke Heller, does an incredibly effective job of teaching us how to witness in a loving, non-threatening way. His approach has been proven to work with friends, family, and associates. Many Christians seem to forget that the last thing Christ commanded us to do (He never made suggestions) was to go into all the world preaching, teaching, baptizing, and making disciples of others. Too many of us are so afraid we will offend someone that we hesitate to approach our own families.

If you know Christ as Lord and the incredible benefits that come with knowing Him, why on earth would you hesitate to share the most important truth in the world with a lost friend or relative?

Dr. Heller has worked for years to perfect his *May I Share?* approach. He has counseled and consulted with wise, knowledgeable people who also love the Lord. He has listened to and used their counsel and advice. Result: he himself has used what he teaches hundreds of times with remarkable results. This has been his passion for years.

I personally have benefited from Dr. Heller's teaching and from my relationship with him. Having known him and his family for many years, I can tell you he has a heart for the lost, a heart for Christ, and a heart for sharing.

As you read this book I encourage you to keep pen and paper handy. As the truths unfold and the processes are burned into your memory, list the names of people you love enough to share the greatest story ever told.

Dr. Heller teaches how to "tell the story," how to share your faith. He emphasizes that you should always ask for a decision simply because you do not know whether that person will be alive the next time you see him or her. He reminds us that if the Holy Spirit has been involved in our efforts, when we do our part, the Holy Spirit will do His. It's not what we do; it's what the Holy Spirit does.

Read this book with joy; read it with commitment. Use what you learn and you'll experience the greatest joy of your life. From personal experience I can share with you that there is no joy equal to that of introducing someone to Christ. This book teaches you a loving, non-threatening, practical way to do exactly that.

Most important, we need to remember that we are the only Bible some people will ever read, so the example we set is critically important. We have to walk the walk as we talk the talk. It's exciting to know that God permits us to have the opportunity to influence people for the Kingdom.

God bless you as you serve our Lord in this most significant way, working with the Holy Spirit to bring people into the Kingdom.

Zig Ziglar
Author, *Over the Top*
Christian Motivational Speaker
Dallas, Texas

"No One Has a More Infectious Enthusiasm"
– Richard Mayhue

Perhaps you can remember when you were saved. For me, it was on a Monday night, April 6, 1970, at Scott Memorial Baptist Church in San Diego. 'B' and I struggled in our three-year-old marriage because I loved my career as a naval officer and she loved our eighteen-month-old daughter. But we had little love for each other.

Fortunately, our Christian neighbors had become friends and started inviting us to their church. Every time, we politely refused. Finally, just to appease them, I said yes to a Monday night family seminar. We figured nothing spectacular could happen on a weekday night at a Baptist church.

That evening we heard a simple gospel presentation. I had heard the gospel before, but it had never made much sense; besides, in my estimation, I really did not live badly enough to be considered a thoroughgoing sinner.

But this time proved different. Everything I heard computed. All that the preacher, Kenny Poure, said had the authority of Scripture. My sinfulness became clear in light of God's holiness—I was lost and needed to be rescued. Christ's death on my behalf and God's offer of eternal life were graciously irresistible. By the end of the service, I figured that the only thing to do was to accept what I so clearly needed and what God had so mercifully provided, and so I did. So did 'B'.

Our neighbors and the preacher loved us enough to initiate "kingdom conversations" about Jesus Christ and our need of His salvation work on the cross. This contemporary pattern actually mimicked an ancient model perfected by Jesus in His earthly ministry.

Note two of His most striking "kingdom conversations."

First, look in on a religiously-oriented person who erroneously believed, as I did at one time, that salvation depended primarily on himself rather than on God. We both centered our hopes on human achievement rather than divine accomplishment.

The rich young ruler, highly interested in life beyond death, ran with urgency to inquire of Jesus publicly, "What shall I do to inherit eternal life?" (Mark 10:17). Our Lord's answer has baffled people through the centuries because He did not respond with a simple, "Believe on Me and you will have eternal life." Rather, He exposed the young man's counterfeit interest.

The inquirer betrayed his apparent sincerity by four common mistakes people make in regard to the true nature of salvation.

First, he would not acknowledge his own spiritual bankruptcy by admitting he could do nothing to merit eternal life (10:17). Only God could accomplish his salvation.

Second, he did not acknowledge the Lord Jesus as God. He saw Him only as a good teacher who could explain the way of God (10:18).

Third, he failed to recognize and repent of his own personal sinfulness (10:19–20). Rather, he extolled the self-righteous virtues of his life from his youth up.

Fourth, he refused to accept the exchanged life of following the will of Christ as Savior and Lord, rather than continuing to pursue his own agenda (10:21–22).

Don't be confused here—Jesus did not teach a salvation by works. Rather, just the opposite. The rich young ruler tried to gain eternal life through human effort; but the Lord, through a series of questions and commands, pointed him to the real heart of true salvation extended by the mercy and grace of God. Receiving the free gift of eternal life involves at least these four elements:

1. Admitting that only God can save us
2. Acknowledging Jesus Christ as God in human flesh
3. Agreeing to our personal sin which needs God's forgiveness
4. Accepting God's terms of salvation.

With a significantly different outcome, never has there been a more classic "kingdom conversation" than the one recorded in John 4. While the rich young ruler sought out Christ, here, Jesus initiated the conversation by simply expressing a single need as a weary traveler to an immoral Samaritan woman, "Give Me a drink." (John 4:6–7). The Lord Jesus quickly turned her attention to another kind of water, living water from an inexhaustible supply that satisfies now and forever with eternal life (4:9–14). She rapidly sensed a thirst for the water that Jesus offered (4:15) and expressed her religious belief in Messiah (4:25). Next, she personally believed Christ's claim to be Messiah and effectively told others about Him (4:28–30). Unlike the rich young ruler who rejected Christ's message, she not only personally embraced it but convincingly told those closest to her.

The results proved remarkable. Many in her hometown believed in Messiah because of the woman's testimony (4:39). And many more believed because of Christ's own teaching during His unexpected, two-day layover (4:40–42). Remember, this spectacular time of evangelism began with the most basic of "kingdom conversations," when Jesus humbly asked, "Give Me a drink."

I know of no one who has a more infectious enthusiasm for following Christ's example of initiating "kingdom conversations" than my long-time friend Duke Heller. For thirty years I have been challenged and inspired by his fearless efforts to present the Lord Jesus Christ to lost and dying people. Therefore, it is a personal delight to commend *How to Start a Kingdom Conversation*, written by a master practitioner. His literary labors provide the necessary motivation, the exclusive message, and the practical method for you, too, to become a kingdom conversationalist—just like our Savior, the Lord Jesus Christ.

Richard Mayhue, Th.D.
Executive Vice President
The Master's College and Seminary
Santa Clarita, California

"Join Duke on This Journey"
– Erwin Lutzer

You hold in your hands a practical book that will help you start a spiritual conversation with practically anyone--including your own relatives!

Duke Heller does not write as a theoretician who tells us how to witness; he takes us by the hand and shows us how to share our faith by examples drawn from his own experience. Here is a man who understands both the gospel and human nature and puts the two together, showing how we can gain legitimate entry into the lives of others. He knows how to open spiritual conversations in a most natural and appealing way. Here is help for us all!

It is my conviction that the reason the early church gained such momentum in the early centuries was that believers shared their faith wherever God planted them. The same can be said for the growth of the church in present-day China, where for decades there has been no freedom of religion. The church has grown for one simple reason: ordinary Christians shared with their coworkers the good news that had transformed them.

If the church in America is to have a greater impact on our culture, it will not be through the media (important though that is) or through massive evangelistic campaigns. It will be because of a revival among common Christians who befriend their neighbors and give an authentic witness to the faith.

Yet, sadly, many Christians find the gap between them and the unconverted so formidable they don't attempt to bridge it. Even when God opens a door to witness, many believers don't know what to say and they bypass the opportunity. Thankfully, in this book, Duke Heller helps us build a bridge to neighbors, relatives—yes even waitresses—in such a way that they are willing to give the gospel a hearing. I've tried some of his suggestions and discovered that they work. You will have the same experience.

I pray that multitudes will read this book and begin to apply its principles and teachings. I'm convinced that those who read these pages and begin to open spiritual conversations with their acquaintances will begin a lifelong journey of joy and spiritual fruitfulness. At last, we again will be a church that impacts our culture with the only message that really matters.

So, join Duke on a journey. Begin reading now, and apply tomorrow what you've read. The God who calls us to witness to His Grace is with us every step of the way.

Erwin W. Lutzer
Moody Church
Chicago, Illinois

"Duke Will Show Us How"
– Jim Custer

You hold in your hands a book that brings together two privileges you have been given. It asks the most important question everyone must answer and the most important people in your life who must answer that question.

If your mother were dying and you could spare her life by donating one of your two kidneys, would you not eagerly give her that gift of life? If you observed signs of critical health problems in your closest friend, would you not urge him or her to seek medical care for those problems? Would you watch your toddler run into the path of a speeding car and not move to save him? If you truly love those in need, and own the power to help them avoid pain and death, you would do it in spite of the personal risk.

These pages offer you encouragement to talk with your closest friends about the questions of death, eternity, and God's offer of the free gift of eternal life. The suggestions have been lab-tested in real-life conversations. They are like seeds which the Spirit of God may bring to your mind as wise resources to guide your conversations toward understanding and response.

However, this book cannot make you start such conversations. That requires obedience. Only the Holy Spirit can put into your heart the passion to share God's good news. He generates this urgency and the courage to initiate the conversation, while you are praying for the "not-sure-they're-saved" in your circle of friends.

Persistent, daily prayer builds your resolve to share, and ignites a desire to initiate a kingdom conversation with the friend. Urgent concern for the eternal health of loved ones flows out of time talking with God about their condition. When you are together in His Throne Room, God will pour His love for them into your soul. He is the Savior; you are the delivery agent. By His wisdom their ignorance is uncovered and solved. Your mind becomes the platform for His assault; your words His delivery system. Conviction of personal sin and fear of coming judgment are not generated in their heart by your clever arguments, but by the Holy Spirit giving them understanding.

Duke's passion for sharing God's gift with others is fueled in his daily prayer meetings with His Lord. This urgency overrides any fears of what people will think about him. It focuses his energies upon what God thinks about his life. He is convinced that God is able to save from sin anyone who will receive by faith His Son, Jesus Christ, as personal Lord and Savior. He writes this book to help you avoid one of the greatest mistakes you will regret for the rest of you life.

God calls us to share our Savior aggressively with those whom we love. How can we watch them perish without telling them about His gift of life and grace through engaging them in a Kingdom Conversation? Duke will show us how.

Jim Custer, Pastor
Grace Brethren Church of Worthington
Columbus, Ohio

Confrontation

"Are you a Christian, Dr. Heller?"

One of my patients asked me this unexpected question. I of course, answered, "Yes, I am!"

"How long have you been a Christian?" was the next question. I boldly replied, "All my life!"

The patient looked me in the eye and said, "You ain't one!"

He then pressed the issue. "Can you point to the exact time you accepted Christ as your Savior?" he asked.

I told him that he certainly did not understand. I was the dentist for the Methodist Children's Home; I did cost-for-materials-only dentistry for some pastors and their wives. I was a family man who loved my wife. I worked hard not to do "wrong things."

Sensing I was defensive, my patient said, "Dr. Heller, please don't take this the wrong way, but you are a fake! A Christian must be able to point to an exact time he accepted Christ or he is playing a game with God."

I was totally taken aback by his boldness. Walking out of the room into the hallway, I asked the hygienist to "please dismiss that kook."

The Rest of the Story

I am sure we would all agree that Mr. Smith's approach is not the best technique for sharing one's faith with a relative or friend. But you need to know the rest of the story. I could not get Mr. Smith's words out of my mind. I commented to the staff about his being one of those "Jesus Freaks." My wife, upon hearing of my day at the office, listened closely as I tried to explain away my answers to him.

Self-Examination

I found myself examining my thoughts during my quiet early morning jogs around the high school track. Why was Mr. Smith so sure of his questions and my replies? I began to ask myself whether I really had enough information to make a spiritual decision. What if I really did not know how to define a true Christian? What if I got to be 50 years old and found that my ladder was leaning against the wrong wall?

I have always been one to pose questions to myself, and my thoughts eventually led me to seek spiritual information for myself. I was happily married with three children, my dental practice was growing, I was having fun coaching little league football and baseball, and my golf game was improving. I was happy with my life. So why couldn't I get Mr. Smith's comments out of my mind? I now know the Holy Spirit was putting a burden on my heart to learn more about God.

I remember one time sitting in the worship service of our church looking religious. While the pastor was preaching, I was using 3" x 6" blue cards for taking notes. But I was not making notes of the sermon! Only my wife Wanda, sitting next to me, knew that I was working on Monday's dental schedule. I don't recall the pastor ever talking about a relationship with God, but a lot of organizing was done during the worship service!

Looking for Help

During the next three to four months after the conversation with my patient, there were times Wanda and I would drop our children off at Sunday school at our regular church, then visit other churches to hear the sermon. One day we visited a Grace Brethren church. As we sat down, the pastor asked the congregation to turn to a New Testament Scripture. Since we did not have a Bible with us, a pleasant lady sitting beside us asked: "Would you like to use my Bible and I'll look on with my friend?" She gave us her Bible, which was turned to the correct passage.

The pastor then instructed us to turn to an additional Scripture in another New Testament book. I looked out of the corner of my eye at the lady sitting beside me and saw she was turning to the left in her Bible. I did likewise, and, to my amazement, I found the book and verse the pastor was discussing. He then asked the audience to turn to a book in the Old Testament. I turned to the left—and to the left—and to the right. Embarrassed, I left the Bible open to a different book from the one the pastor referred to and acted interested. I tried on two different occasions to follow the pastor's Scripture readings. Finally, I closed the Bible in disgust and embarrassment.

I was impressed with the warm feeling in the congregation, but I felt we would probably not return because I could not follow the pastor's Scripture search. (Any excuse will work if you are looking for one.) I told Wanda afterward that those people scared me to death. I naturally classified the church members as a bunch of "Jesus Freaks." Wanda informed me she really liked the pastor, and the people were very warm. She added, "I'll bet they have a nice program for the children."

The next Sunday we prepared to return to our regular church. My daughter, Kerry, was wearing a nice yellow dress and carrying a brown paper bag. When I inquired about the bag, she informed me it was "blue jeans for Sunday school." As Wanda and I were sitting in the worship service that morning, I had a nagging feeling about Kerry and her bag with blue jeans. I told Wanda I was going downstairs to check out Kerry's Sunday school class. When I peeked in the door of her class, I saw about ten girls standing on their heads! All of them were wearing blue jeans. Their dresses were down over their heads and faces. Their arms were folded; their heads held all of their weight. Their eyes were closed and the room was quiet.

"What are we doing here?" I asked the teacher. She told me the class was studying yoga. "When do they study the Bible?" I inquired. "Next quarter," the teacher replied. I went back upstairs and told Wanda we were going to leave this church.

We went to other churches, but my mind went back to the love and friendliness of the Grace Brethren church and the people I had criticized as being "Jesus Freaks." The week before Easter, 1972, we returned for another visit. That morning Pastor Jim Custer preached a sermon on death and one's relationship with Christ. He made a startling analogy about having a teenage child die and knowing for sure where the child would be after death. He said, "I don't mean someone in the reception line would come and tell you that your child was in a better place. I mean, do you know, one-hundred-percent-for-sure, your child would be in a better place?"

Knowing for Sure

His words drove a spike into my heart. Kerry was thirteen years old. I had to admit if I looked in her casket, I would not know for sure where she would be in the spiritual realm.

Pastor Jim then said, "If you do not know where your teenage daughter would be, there is a good chance you don't know where you would be, as well." He then gave an invitation to come forward to the front of the church.

I excused myself and walked forward. Associate Pastor Frank Gardner came to meet me. He looked at me, and I looked at him. I did not know what to say. Finally Pastor Gardner said, "Is there an area of your life you want to turn over to God?"

"Yes, that's it!" I said.

He led me into another room. "Your name again?" he asked.

I replied, "Duke Heller."

"Well, Duke, how long have you known the Lord?"

"All my life!" I replied.

Pastor Gardner's eyes widened. He said, "What? You can't point to a time in your life when you accepted Christ?"

"No sir, I cannot," I replied.

"Would you like to do it now?" he asked.

I eagerly replied, "Yes, sir. I definitely would like to do it now."

I explained that a few months before, a patient had also confronted me, and his words had bothered me ever since. I asked what I had to do to make sure I had accepted Christ as my Savior.

Pastor Gardner informed me that I should include three items in my prayer to God. First, I needed to admit I was a sinner. "You do admit you are a sinner, don't you?" he asked bluntly. I assured him that I agreed.

He told me I also needed to ask Jesus Christ to forgive me of my sins, and to ask Him to become Lord of my life.

I was hoping Pastor Gardner would pray the salvation prayer and I would pray after him, but he told me I needed to pray out loud using my own words. That was the day I accepted Christ.

I strongly believe that God took me down a life path with my patient's challenge. The purpose of this book is to give you hope and direction in boldly sharing your faith with those closest to you. It will give you suggestions for entering into a spiritual conversation and provide step-by-step techniques for presenting your faith. These are proven techniques that are non-threatening. This book will help you overcome fear when sharing with those you love. God can use anything we say, but He can't use our silence.

CHAPTER 1

No Regrets!

*"The bitterest tears shed over graves
are for words left unsaid and
deeds left undone."*

~Harriett Beecher Stowe (1811-1896)

Kingdom Conversations

I was mowing my parents' lawn one day in 1985 when my sister Edna called. Her husband, Harry, had been diagnosed with liver cancer some time before. Now she informed me that he had taken a turn for the worse.

I had already asked my sister and others about Harry's relationship with Christ. Their standard reply was that Harry was a Christian. When I asked how they knew, they responded that he was raised in the church and definitely believed in God.

I showered and headed for Harry and Edna's house. There I found my sister and their three daughters standing at the foot of Harry's bed. I could tell that Harry was weak and life was draining from him. I sat down on the bed beside him and said, "Harry, they tell me you are getting worse and are going to die. Are you sure you are going to heaven when you die?"

"I hope so," Harry replied.

"Would you like to make absolutely sure that you are going to heaven?" I asked.

"Yes, I would," Harry replied. I then asked Harry, "Do you believe you are a sinner?" Harry admitted he was a sinner. I then said, "Can you point to an exact time that you accepted Christ as your Savior?" "No, I cannot remember doing it," Harry whispered. I then asked Harry if he was willing to pray out loud at that very moment and admit he was a sinner, to ask Jesus Christ to forgive him of his sins, and ask Christ to become Lord of his life.

Harry prayed the sinners' prayer and squeezed my hand tightly as his breath was almost gone. He told me he was happy he had done what was necessary to go to heaven.

My sister and her three daughters stood at the end of the bed and heard their husband and father accept Christ on his deathbed. My sister had accepted Christ in 1983, and the Holy Spirit was not calling any of her three daughters at the time. As of the writing of this book, I have no assurance of her daughters' making a personal commitment. I was informed that one of the daughters told my sister, "I can't believe Uncle Duke would tell dad he was going to die and that he needed to pray *now.*" Of course, my sister is glad today that her husband prayed that prayer, as he died soon after our talk about the Lord. We will have an opportunity to be with Harry in the future.

My father-in-law, Hubert Rogers, whom we affectionately called Buck, was diagnosed with liver cancer the next year. He was a great father-in-law. It was through him and his family that I learned it was okay for a man to hug another man. Buck taught me to play golf when I was in college. We would play together summers when I was home from college.

When I learned that Buck had cancer, I inquired about his relationship with the Lord. Members of his family told me that he knew Christ as his Savior. When I asked, "When did he accept Christ?" I was not pleased with the answer and decided to find out for myself.

Wanda and I were home for the Christmas holidays in 1986. Buck was looking forward to the grandchildren's coming to his house for Christmas. He was very sick and in bed. I went into his bedroom to talk to him.

"Buck, they tell me you are really sick and the medicine is not working as expected. If you don't make it through this disease, when you get to heaven and God says, 'Why should I let you in?' what are you going to say?"

Buck quickly told me that he believed in Jesus Christ as his personal Savior. I asked him, "Can you point to an exact time that you accepted Christ?"

Buck told me that he had accepted Christ as a youth and told me how it happened. I talked to him at length about spiritual things. Later I felt very comfortable telling people that I was sure Buck knew the Lord. Buck had not been upset, as some might expect, but was happy to discuss his salvation. A red flag goes up in my mind when someone resists telling me about his date of salvation. People who get upset need to re-evaluate their relationship with Christ. As a believer, I would consider it an honor if someone cared enough about me to ask me personally about Christ before I asked them about Christ. Buck went home to be with the Lord just after Christmas. I felt comfortable looking in his casket, knowing that our conversation had confirmed in my mind his position in Christ.

When you attend the funeral of a loved one, what will you be thinking as you look into the casket? I, for one, want to be confident the individual in the casket had sufficient information clearly presented to him that gave him the opportunity to accept Jesus Christ as his personal Savior.

Many people would agree that family is the most important aspect of life. We would probably rate our spouse and children as our highest priority. We would also include our other relatives—our mother, father, sisters, brothers, aunts, uncles, grandmothers, grandfathers, and cousins—as our next priority. If we are concerned about our relatives' relationships with Christ, we need to pray for them by name and systematically set up times to share the Gospel with them.

Since the Holy Spirit is the only person who can draw an individual to Himself, we should force ourselves to be the messenger and leave the results to Him. If you are uncomfortable in sharing your faith, you can learn to get out of your comfort zone! God wants you to become involved in the spiritual lives of your relatives.

Starting a Conversation

To start a kingdom conversation, ask, "How is your life?" instead of "How are you?" or "How are you doing?" The first question requires an answer. The last two questions usually just get a response of "OK."

"How is your life?" is a great question to ask your relatives, since you already know them, but may need to be brought up to date with their present life situations and the trials of their lives.

Remember, your ultimate goal is to find a way to switch the present conversation to a kingdom discussion. Therefore, you must always listen to the answers to your questions. You must be interested in how your relative responds.

Once you have heard the person's answer, follow up with, "How are you doing with (insert something they told you about, such as the loss of their job or a report of cancer or their son's illness)?"

After hearing of a concern worthy of prayer, one of the best "lead-ins" for a spiritual conversation is: "I have been praying for…." Nothing gets to spiritual involvement faster than telling them you are praying for their problem, if in fact you are praying for them. But don't lie. God is keeping score!

If you have not been praying for their particular problem or situation, say, "With your permission, may I pray for …?" By offering to pray for them, you have immediately taken the conversation to a spiritual level. Take out a piece of paper, write down the prayer request and add it to your prayer list. If you don't already have a prayer list—start one!

Don't offer to pray unless you really will pray regularly for them and their present problem or concern. They will know you have been praying if you ask them about the situation the next time you see them.

To get even more input, you might say, "I have been praying for your son's illness. How can I best pray for him?"

Your relative knows that you care because you are praying for his or her son. You also are going to get the latest update on the problem by finding out how to best pray for that person or a member of the person's family.

To get the conversation to an even deeper level you might ask, "How are you handling that situation?"

Get to Involvement Quickly

Once you have opened the conversation, get involved. Ask questions like,

"How can I help you with…?"

"With whom are you counseling about…?" (Be aware that most men don't seek counsel.)

"What outcome would you like to see happen with…?"

"Is God part of your decision making process? How?"

"Do you feel comfortable calling on God for help?"

Jesus made statements or asked questions that required answers. Your questions should call for answers that will lead to a spiritual conversation. Many times, by asking these questions, you will have enough information to help you lead into an opportunity to share the gospel.

Determining Their Spiritual Status

You might say, "May I share with you how God has helped me overcome similar problems in my own life?" Then use examples from your life to show how God has helped you in a difficult situation. Nobody can criticize you for what God has done in your life!

Then you might ask, "Do you think God hears every prayer of people in distress?" If they seem unsure, ask, "What do you think of God?" Let them talk—everyone has some opinion on God.

The Permission Question

Once they have exchanged thoughts by answering questions and telling you what they think about God, you may want to use the following sentence, which is very easy to say:

"May I share something with you that someone once shared with me that made it easier for me to understand who God is?"

This statement is non-threatening because it is stated in a third-party context. How can Person A be offended if Person B wants to share something that Person C told Person B? This is very useful with relatives because they are usually eager to help their relatives better understand life's deep questions. You can then use one of the techniques from Chapters 6 through 8 to share Christ, or use your personal testimony to explain how Christ saved you. In Chapter 6 I will explain how to use the *Mayishare* brochure effectively.

We must have a special urgency for sharing Christ with our relatives. It's so easy for the routines of life to get in the way, and we put off until tomorrow what we should have done today. When the telephone call comes, explaining that Aunt Jane had a massive heart attack and died last night, you will not be able to forget that you put off going to visit her because you assumed you had plenty of time to do it.

Let's now look at how to share Christ with your closest and most important relatives—your parents.

CHAPTER 2

Approaching our Parents

Most of us would probably agree that there is more urgency to share Christ with our mother and father than with anyone else, because of our love for them and their advancing age. Even if we have not had the best relationship with our parents in the past, we recognize that our parents probably did the best they could in raising us with the help they got from their parents' background. Many books on parenting are now available, But we cannot be too critical of our parents, who likely did not have parenting books or seminars to use in raising us.

If your relationship with your parents has been broken or damaged, keep in mind that your mother and father were chosen by God to bring you into this world. Who knows your parents better than you do? Who is more indebted to them than you? Your taking the initiative to rebuild a relationship with your parents may allow you to share spiritual information with them in the future. Perhaps a written thank-you letter could start to rebuild the relationship. Your effort may give them the opportunity to make the decision about Christ that will allow them to spend eternity with you.

Make an Opportunity

The following technique worked for me, and it has worked for many others who have used this sincere approach with their parents.

You owe it to yourself and to them to try it. This approach will work even if you have attempted to communicate spiritual knowledge with them in the past or if you feel you have "messed up" your gospel presentation to them.

Call your parents on the phone if they live fairly close, inviting them to your home for lunch. Plan to have the grandchildren busy after lunch so you can talk sincerely and quietly with your parents.

Here's how I approached my parents.

"Mom, Dad, I have something that is very important to me that I really want to share with you. I love you both very much and realize you love me as well. You have brought me up to realize that honesty and integrity are admirable qualities. As you know, God is very important to me and I want to teach godly principles and knowledge to your grandchildren.

"Wanda and I have prayed that God would direct us as we raise our family with these godly principles. May I go over this information with you so you will know why I am excited about using this knowledge and these principles to help raise your grandchildren?"

This should put your parents in a receptive mode, showing them why this conversation is important to you—to help you raise your children in a godly manner. If you do not have children, then you can say "to have a godly marriage." If you are not married, you can say "to lead a godly life."

Ask Permission to Share

Now you can ask that important question, "May I share something with you that someone once shared with me that made it easier for me to understand who God is?" By progressing into a third party discussion, you can next say; "My friend asked me, '(insert your name), when you die and go to heaven and God asks, "Why should I let you in?" what are you going to say?'"

You can then draw your parents into the conversation by asking them the same questions your friend asked you and getting their replies. I described how I went forward in church and explained the three things I told God: 1) I am a sinner; 2) Christ, please forgive my sins; 3) Christ, will you please become Lord of my life and allow me to live the life you would want me to live?

Closing the Deal

It is very important to make sure you "close the deal" in your conversation. Many Christians have the opportunity to share their faith with their parents, but fail to take the next crucial step. They do not ask their parents to make a verbal decision *at that moment* for Jesus Christ.

I asked my parents two closing questions:

"Mom, Dad, does this information make sense to you?"

"Mom, Dad, is there any reason you would not want to accept Jesus Christ at this time?"

Their answers to these two questions gave me permission to ask the most important question.

Make Sure!

This experience is certainly a wasted effort if you accept answers like: "I am a Christian," "I believe in Christ," or "I memorized Scripture when I was going to church." The most important question to ask at this point is, "Mom, Dad, can you point to an exact time you prayed the prayer to accept Christ?"

If the person has previously prayed to accept Jesus Christ as personal Savior, they should be able to point to the exact date of the salvation prayer. If the person answers, "Yes," say, "Tell me about it!" Asking your parent to tell their story will allow you the opportunity to evaluate carefully whether he or she has in fact prayed the prayer or is merely playing a game with words. Born-again Christians do not mind how many times they are asked about the exact date of their salvation.

Sometimes our parents, relatives, or friends will say, "I can't point to a certain date, but I have done it." Again, you can say: "Tell me about it!" As they tell you about the circumstances of the prayer or situation, you must pray silently, asking the Holy Spirit to help you discern for sure whether they have truly made a commitment to Christ. Many people cannot tell you an exact date, but they can tell you the circumstances, such as:

"I was five years old and I asked my mother what I had to do to keep from going to hell."

"I went forward at a youth camp and prayed the prayer to accept Christ as my Savior when I was eleven or twelve or maybe even thirteen years old."

Ask them: "Do you remember praying the prayer telling Christ you were a sinner and asking Him to forgive you of your sins?" By asking your relative to point to an exact time and then asking him or her to tell you about the circumstances, you overcome the vague answer.

Nothing could be more cruel to your relative than for you to accept an answer that satisfied your conversation but did not hold up to God's salvation standard. God accepts only true confessions of a repentant sinner, not words that sound good but are without repentance.

Neither of my parents accepted Christ the first time I shared the gospel with them. My mother was raised a Methodist and felt that was sufficient to be a Christian. My father, to my knowledge, was in a church only when his children were married and at funerals. He and my mother were married by a justice of the peace in a courthouse. He was quiet the first time I shared the gospel with them. As I recall, my mother did most of the talking.

Two weeks later, my mother called and asked if they could come over and discuss "that religious stuff again." I was, of course, excited that they now wanted to talk about it. But if my parents had died before they had called back to discuss it more, I would have been satisfied looking into their caskets knowing I had shared the Gospel. I had given them enough information to make a decision for Christ.

Naturally, I was thrilled when they returned in two weeks. After sitting through the entire discussion again, both decided to accept Christ by praying the "repentant prayer."

I would encourage you to consider having this conversation with your parents, and possibly with all of your unsaved relatives. Your parents, however, are a must. Contact them first. If you have a specific situation that makes you feel uncomfortable using the above wording or technique, please feel free to call me at (614) 888-4830. I feel confident that after thirty years I have encountered most conversation situations. I would be honored to talk with you and help you use wording that perhaps will make it easier for you to share Christ with your relatives.

I once heard a story that illustrates this point. A young boy was having a hard day. His mother was unhappy with him, his best friend did not want to play with him, and his dog was not acting friendly. Feeling sorry for himself, he decided to walk along the beach. As he walked, he saw hundreds of starfish washed up on the sand because of a bad storm. In the distance, he noticed an older man picking up something and throwing it back in the water.

As he got closer, he realized the older man was throwing washed-up starfish back into the water. Approaching the man, he said in a nasty voice, "What are you doing? You can't make a difference with the hundreds of starfish that washed up on the sand." The old gentleman reached down and picked up another starfish, tossing it far out into the ocean. "It makes a difference to that one," he said.

You can make a difference to your unsaved parent or relative!

We all have relatives who have washed up on the shore of life. You are one of the people God has chosen to make a difference in their lives! Put these relatives on your salvation prayer list immediately, and then call them to set up a time to visit. You can't afford to be too busy....do it *now!*

As the Nike commercial urges, "Just do it!" I understand that the verb from which "nike" comes in Greek can mean "conqueror, victor, overcomer."

In the next chapter I'll tell you about some specific people I shared Christ with, and a bit of the story of what happened with them.

CHAPTER 3

Am I My Brother's Keeper?

I was speaking to a fairly large Sunday school class with a mixture of parents, teenagers, and college students. One girl in the audience had gone to a Christian school from kindergarten through twelfth grade. She was currently a sophomore at a Christian college, home for the holidays.

When I teach people how to share their faith, I purposely walk around the room, pointing my finger at individuals, exclaiming, "Can *you* point to the exact time? Can *you* point to the exact time?" I emphasize "you" and look directly into their eyes.

As I moved about the room, I got a funny feeling about this girl. My eyes met hers and I felt something as our eyes met. Later that afternoon I was sitting at home reading when the telephone rang. It was her father. He told me that she had just accepted Christ in her bedroom. She said that when I continued to ask the question, "Can you point to the exact time?" she realized that she could not do it. That bothered her. Since she could not point to a time, she knew she needed to do it now!

Her parents informed me that they would have been willing to bet half their house that she already knew the Lord. She grew up in the church. She was a great kid; she memorized Scripture. Can you imagine the pain those parents might have experienced in heaven if they were walking the golden streets without their daughter? God is good—but we have to ask the question.

Not Knowing for Sure

Another time, I was invited to speak to a group of dentists in Chicago. Pat picked me up at the airport and informed me he was also picking up another speaker, Craig, who was coming in on the next plane. I had made plans to go to dinner with Gil, a former student of mine. Gil was struggling with some life issues and had e-mailed me, asking for an opportunity to talk about those issues. Since I was leaving the following day after speaking, I knew I would have to talk to Gil that evening. Now, unfortunately, there were going to be four people at dinner together.

Gil and I sat on the same side of a booth, talking periodically about a few of his challenges. I knew that Gil felt religious and was trying to please God by attending church—often. The meal was served around 11:00 pm, which was midnight my time. We did not finish eating until 11:45.

It was obvious to me that Gil needed a personal relationship with Christ. Therefore, I took the available opportunity. Turning toward Gil, I asked that key question, "May I share something with you that someone once shared with me that made it easier for me to understand who God is and how God was able to help me solve some similar problems?"

Gil responded that the information would be welcome. While Pat and Craig carried on a separate conversation, I acted as if Gil were the only person present at the table. Gil and I looked each other in the eye, discussing the contents of the *Mayishare* brochure, my preferred method of sharing. He willingly answered the important questions discussed in the brochure.

When we got to the section that asks, "Can you point to an exact time that you accepted Christ as your Savior?" Gil told me he could not. I then asked, "Gil, does this information make sense to you?" He replied affirmatively. "Is there any reason you would not want to pray to accept Christ *now*—here in this restaurant?" By this time, Pat and Craig were listening to our conversation.

Gil replied that he would like to pray immediately! Gil prayed the sinners' prayer, and then I prayed, thanking God for choosing Gil on that special night in that restaurant.

I immediately turned to Craig, "Can *you* point to an exact time that you accepted Christ?"

Craig said he remembered my sharing the same information with him several years before. He had not accepted Christ at that time, but he informed me he had done so at a recent Easter service at his church. I then asked Pat the same question about his knowing an exact date.

Pat replied, "Don't you remember when you shared Christ with me? It was at a Popeye's chicken restaurant in Cincinnati."

"I remember exactly when you accepted Christ," I told Pat. "I just wanted to make sure you still remembered!"

Gil later called me and said he thinks he remembers praying the sinner's prayer before, but since praying in the restaurant, he is now "really turned on for Christ and excited to share his faith with his friends and patients." Whether Gil had done it before or not, he was willing that day to make sure in the restaurant.

Prepared Hearts

Another incident confirms the importance of asking that crucial question about the exact time a person accepted Christ. A Texas dentist asked me to meet him and a friend, to find out where his friend stood with the Lord. After some small talk, I asked the friend, "Living in Texas, you were fortunate to grow up in the Bible belt. Which church did you and your family attend?" He said he was raised Baptist, but he did not regularly attend any more. When I asked why he did not attend regularly, his reply was that there were "too many hypocrites" in the church.

I asked if I could share with him what someone else had shared with me that made it easier for me to understand God better. He allowed me to go through the *Mayishare* brochure, step by step.

Halfway through the brochure conversation, Charles, a Jewish dentist from New York City, asked to sit with us for breakfast. I invited him to sit down and listen to my attempt to help my new friend understand why God was important to me. When we got to the end of the brochure, I asked the friend of the Texan dentist if he could point to an exact time he accepted Christ. "Yes, as a teenager," he said.

"Tell me about it!" I interjected immediately.

He told of a boyhood decision that sounded sincere and truthful to me. My Texan dentist friend, who asked me to share with this individual, was shocked. He said, "Really? You have committed your life to Christ? I sure am glad to hear that, as I have been wondering for the last ten years."

An Unprepared Heart

I immediately turned to Charles and asked him, "Can *you* point to a time in your life concerning a personal relationship with Jesus Christ?"

"I have a different belief system. I am part of the chosen people line," he said. "We believe the Messiah has not come yet."

I asked if he would be willing to meet me and discuss it. He agreed to meet. At our breakfast table after the other people had left, Charles and I found ourselves alone. I asked him, "Is God part of your decision making process? Your wife has recently been told she has cancer. Are you praying to God to help your wife? Do you think God answers prayer?"

I told him of my belief and that I sincerely wanted him to accept Christ as his Savior. He has since told me he and his wife have attended a church in New York, other than the Jewish synagogue, to ask for God's leadership.

Wanda and I recently went to New York City to have a meeting about an upcoming dental conference. During our time with Charles, I again talked to him about the importance of making a decision for Jesus Christ. I told him that since he was ten years older than I, there was a good chance I would be attending his funeral. I did not want anyone saying to me that I did not give Charles enough information to make a decision for Christ.

Charles turned to me, with a smile on his face, saying, "Duke, nobody will ever be able to say you did not give me enough information about Christ."

I told him, "Charles, this conversation will be played for you again as you attempt to gain entrance into heaven."

I often think of the Texan dentist who spent ten years without knowing his friend was a believer. I was truly privileged to ask the questions. I really like my dentist friend from Texas and felt honored that he asked me to confront his friend. But I wonder why he had to wait until coming to Chicago for a stranger like me to confront his friend. Isn't it funny how we don't want to ask our friends about their relationship with Christ, finding it easier to ask others to help us?

Reaching our friends and acquaintances is one of the greatest privileges and responsibilities we can have. We should take advantage of every opportunity to reach them. Many people desperately need the love and assurance that Christ offers and are open to hearing if we will only turn the conversation that direction.

A Softened Heart

A very wealthy patient of mine came in for his yearly dental check-up. He was part-owner of several large department stores and very stoic in his presence and conversation. Being a very positive individual, I came bounding into the operatory, and in a loud voice said, "Mr. L., How is your life?"

He replied in a soft voice, "Fine."

"Come on, you can do better than that! Let's try that again," I said loudly.

He replied that it was difficult for him to be upbeat with all that was going on with his life. He went on to explain that his wife had just been diagnosed with terminal cancer.

I immediately expressed my sorrow for him and his wife. But I also took the opportunity to say, "With your permission, may I pray for your wife?"

Taking a prescription pad, tearing off a sheet and turning it over to the plain side, I said, "What is her first name? How can I best pray for her?"

I noticed a tear in his eye as I wrote down her name. I touched his arm and said, "I know this must be very difficult for you. Many times shedding tears will help us relieve our emotions."

He replied that life had dealt his family a bad blow. Then he explained that his tear was not for the unexpected trial in his and his wife's lives. He told me what had brought the tear to his eye: "I cannot remember when another male has promised to pray for me or a member of my family!"

Can you imagine my reaction? This seventy-five-year-old man, who had all the material wealth possible, did not have another male friend in his life who ever offered to pray for him or a member of his family! You are blessed if you have people who regularly pray for you and your family. Don't take that lightly.

Do use prayer as a witnessing tool. Obviously, I was by now into a spiritual conversation with my patient friend and had the opportunity to take the conversation in any direction that seemed appropriate.

The Imperative to Share the Gospel

Before we go further, we must recognize that the Bible makes it clear we have a responsibility to reach others. Here are some verses to consider (italics mine):

"For we must all appear before the judgment seat of Christ, that each one may be recompensed for his deeds in the body, according to *what he has done,* whether good or bad" (2 Corinthians 5:10).

"Now this I say, he who *sows sparingly* will also *reap sparingly;* and he who sows bountifully will also reap bountifully" (2 Corinthians 9:6).

"Do not be deceived, God is not mocked; for *whatever a man sows,* this he will *also reap*" (Galatians 6:7).

"He who *watches the wind* will not sow and he who looks at the clouds will not reap" (Ecclesiastes 11:4).

"[D]o not merely look out for your own personal interests, but also for the *interests of others*" (Philippians 2: 4).

"[F]or it is God who is at *work in you,* both to will and to work for His good pleasure" (Philippians 2:13).

"I *planted,* Apollos *watered,* but God was causing the *growth*" (1 Corinthians 3:6).

"For I am not ashamed of the gospel, for it is the power of God for salvation to every one who believes, to the Jew first and also to the Greek" (Romans 1:16).

"The fruit of the righteous is a tree of life, and he who is wise wins souls" (Proverbs 11:30).

We may have intentions to share our faith, but unless we put our foot on the gas pedal and move the car (initiative to share the gospel), the car only races its motor and goes nowhere. As I remind people in my seminars, "God don't move no parked cars!"

Now let's look at an easy formula for asking the right questions to get a kingdom conversation started.

CHAPTER 4

Asking the Right Questions

To reach our friends and neighbors, we can use a similar approach to the one we use with our relatives. Since we already know them, we don't need to worry about trying to break the ice like we would with a stranger. We usually already know something about them and their present life situations.

Most people want a relationship with their neighbors or friends. A conversation formula that will help you get more involved in your neighbor's life involves asking questions based on FORM:

Form

Family
Occupation
Recreation/Retirement
Motivation/Money

Asking questions about these values in your neighbor's life can give you opportunities to lead easily into a spiritual conversation. Here are some examples and practical applications.

Family

Learn the person's name, as well as the spouse's name. Write down their names and store them for later reference. Use the person's name in conversations: "Well, Bill, tell me about...."

Find out the children's names and their activities, too. Ask questions such as, "Are your children involved in soccer?" or "Does Billy like soccer?"

Ask about the person's childhood. "Where did you grow up? Where are you from originally?" "How do you like (your city) compared to...?" Show interest in their relationship: "How did you and your spouse meet?"

Occupation

Inquiring about their occupation is another great opening to provide opportunities for a spiritual conversation. "Where do you work?""What type of work do you do?" "Where does your spouse work?" Learn about their likes/dislikes about their present job. "Do you enjoy your work? Why?"

Recreation/Retirement

To find out the person's recreational interests, ask questions such as, "What are your hobbies?" Is the person involved in neighborhood activities such as scouting, coaching little league teams, or church activities? Ask, "Do you have time to get involved with coaching your children in their activities?" Take advantage of opportunities to build the relationships. Asking "What do you enjoy doing as a family?" may lead you to know that they like picnics, giving you an opportunity to ask, "Would you enjoy going on a picnic with our family?"

If your neighbor is retired, ask questions such as, "How do you and your spouse spend your time?" You can also ask, "Are you able to do any volunteering at your church or a hospital?" "What are your hobbies?" "What exercise do you do consistently?" "Are there activities you and your spouse do together?"

Motivation

Find out what makes your neighbor or friend tick. Ask questions like, "How do you spend most of your after-work hours?" "If making money for your family were not an issue, what would you really like to do?"

What excites him? Look for what turns his motor on with "What do you really like to do?" He may be an accountant by day but work on car motors in his spare time.

Find out his personal or career goals. "Do you and your wife have specific goals for your house?" "What are your goals for your family?"

Money

Find out how important money is to your neighbor. Use questions like, "It sure is difficult to make ends meet in these times, isn't it?" or "Are you able to spend as much time with your family you'd like, or do your office commitments make that difficult?"

Is he or she overextended with work hours? Overwork usually is done for money. You can then ask, "What would you do if you won the lottery?" That tells you what motivates the person.

Ask about plans for the future, "Do you find it hard to save for retirement?" "What plan have you made to help supplement your retirement?"

More Hints for Using FORM

As you ask the FORM questions, be sure to remember what your friend or neighbor tells you. The goal of FORM is to find a way to share the gospel. As you use FORM,

- Be sincerely interested in him as a person and in his life.
- Listen intently to his answers.
- Write down answers on a 3 x 5 card. (A dull pencil is sharper than the sharpest memory).
- Look for an opening to get with him one-on-one eventually.
- Use an approach that is non-threatening, both to you and to him.

One-on-One Conversation

If you found an immediate need or problem when asking one of the FORM questions, consider saying: "With your permission, may I add you (or your situation) to my prayer list?" Or, "How could I best pray for that situation?" Take out a pad and pencil to write down the prayer request. Remember that writing the prayer request in front of the person shows you are sincere in asking to pray for him or her.

Other Lead-in Questions

"Where do you take your children to Sunday school?" This question is a lot less direct than asking people "Where do you attend church?" Many people will answer directly, telling you where they go to church, while others might say they take their children to church only on special occasions, such as Easter or Christmas.

You might also ask, "Do your children enjoy Sunday school?" This could be another way to move the conversation toward spiritual thoughts. After talking about their church and where they take their children to Sunday school, it may be appropriate to ask: "What do you think about God?"

Listen carefully and look in their eyes to get a true reaction. This question can be presented in such a way that it is not confrontational. By simply inquiring about their thoughts on God, we give them an opportunity to express their feelings about a subject that most people avoid. Remember, everybody has an opinion about God. Just listen. I don't tell them I disagree with their comments. One of my favorite replies, if I think their opinion is incorrect, is just, "That is interesting!"

Once they have given me their opinion of who they think God is, they have given me the right to tell them what I think about God. If I wait a few minutes, they will often ask, "Duke, what do you think about God?" This, of course, gives me an opportunity to use the third party, non-threatening approach: "May I share something with you that someone once shared with me that made it easier for me to understand who God is?"

I once heard a sermon by Pastor Lee Strobel on a Focus on the Family radio broadcast entitled, "What If Jesus Lived in My House?" Much of the four points that follow are from that sermon and are used here by permission.

How Would Jesus Act? What Would Jesus Do?

Before Jesus would talk to His neighbor about His heavenly Father, He would talk to His heavenly Father *about* His neighbor. Jesus would pray fervently for His lost neighbor. Jesus prayed up until His death for the lost. His last words were, "Forgive them, Father, for they know not what they do." Jesus would let His neighbor know His door would always be open for any question. He would always be willing to change His schedule to accommodate His lost neighbor.

Peter tells us "always [be] ready to make a defense to every one who asks you to give an account for the hope that is in you, yet with gentleness and reverence . . ." (1 Peter 3:15)

Jesus would not only share His faith, but He would show His faith. He would back up His faith with actions of serving His lost neighbor. Jesus served the lepers by healing; He served the wedding party by turning water into wine; He served the hungry on a hillside by feeding 5,000.

Matthew 5:16 tells us, "Let your light shine before men in such a way that they may see your good works, and glorify your Father who is in heaven." Humble acts of serving crack open the hardness of a heart. Serve neighbors by shoveling snow, babysitting for a single mom in the neighborhood, or by talking with an elderly person who is lonely.

If Jesus lived in your neighborhood, His antennae would be up to find opportunities to serve His neighbor. Jesus would show a consistency between His beliefs and His behavior—He would live with integrity. He would realize that His neighbor's hypercritical radar would be scanning His life.

Unsaved neighbors are looking for a way to reject you and the church you represent. You might appear spiritual in public, but in private be abusive to your wife, your children, and your dog. Unsaved neighbors are looking to match what you say with what you do—they are not looking for perfect people, but real people. Neighbors need to hear real Christian people talk about real life and learn how God is part of their real lives.

Are you too busy doing ministry in your church to let your neighbor see Jesus in you? Do you represent Christ to your neighbors by being consistent in your actions behind closed doors, or do you scream at your spouse or children? Do you hit the wall with your fist in frustration before going to church, and then drive to church like nothing happened? You may be putting up a good appearance for your children, but they know!

The Apostle Paul states, "[F]or He says, 'At the acceptable time I listened to you, and on the day of salvation I helped you'; behold, now is 'the acceptable time,' behold, now is 'the day of salvation'" (2 Corinthians 6:2).

Paul emphasized his point by quoting Isaiah 49:8. He was passionately concerned that the Corinthians adhere to the truth because it was God's time to save, and they were envoys for helping to spread that message—just as you and I are messengers today. Paul used "the day of salvation" to illustrate that there is a time in God's economy when He listens to sinners and responds to those who are repentant. It was that time then, and it is that time now.

Jesus warned, "We must work the works of Him who sent Me, as long as it is day; night is coming, when no man can work" (John 9:4). There will come a time when the people we want to share our faith with either will not listen, or God will have hardened their hearts. Or they could die unexpectedly. It is urgent that we share the Gospel soon!

Having discussed how to start kingdom conversations with those closest to you, let's now look at how to get into a spiritually meaningful conversation with strangers.

CHAPTER 5

Starting a Conversation with Strangers

Zig Ziglar and I were looking forward to playing golf together at The Memorial Golf Course in Columbus, Ohio, but God had other plans for us. The greens on that course had developed a fungus, so we switched to my favorite Columbus course, The Golf Club, invited by Bill Price. It proved to be an appointment arranged by God.

After finishing our eighteen holes, Zig and I thanked the caddy for his help. As the caddy put our golf clubs into the back of my car, I asked him a sensitive question, "Luke, if you died and went to heaven today and God asked you why He should let you in, what would you say?"

Luke looked at Zig, and then at me, and said, "I heard you guys out there talking about that God stuff. I really don't need that stuff because I have my life all together. I have a degree in philosophy and have found my niche in life being a caddy."

Zig then offered to give him a couple of free tickets to hear General Norman Schwartzkopf, Barbara Bush, and other famous people speak. He did not mention himself, though he also was to be a speaker on that program. Luke thanked him, but said, "I really am happy with my life and don't need any more input. Thanks anyway."

I felt the Holy Spirit was not calling us to witness further to Luke that day, but I decided to give him one of the *Mayishare* brochures. "Will you please look at this brochure and see if any of these questions are of interest to you?" I asked him. He kindly (we had not yet given him a tip) replied that he would read it. I would have bet half my house that he would not read it—but then, he just might.

It's God's Plan

The next day I got a call from the caddy master of The Golf Club. He asked if I was the guy who had given Luke a brochure about God. I replied, "Yes. Why do you ask?"

He then took about fifteen minutes to tell me that Luke had come into the caddy area and thrown the brochure on the table, telling him, "Here is a brochure that might interest you. You're always looking for ways to improve your life."

The caddy master stuck the brochure in his pocket. Later, reading it slowly, he came to the picture with the caption, "Can you point to an exact time you accepted Christ as your Savior?" He could not, so he turned the brochure over, noting the instructions about how to become a Christian.

He told me that he read the three items about becoming a Christian: agreeing he was a sinner, asking Christ to forgive him of his sins, and asking Christ to become Lord of his life. He joyfully told me he had just gotten on his knees and prayed the sinner's prayer. He called to thank me for giving the caddy the brochure. Together, we cried with joy over the phone.

I hung up the receiver, tears running down my face. I realized that God did not use me to reach our caddy, but He used the brochure to reach the caddy's boss. I called Zig with the exciting news. "Are you going back to the caddy, Duke?" Zig asked. He always wants to bring one more into the Kingdom.

This incident illustrates an important lesson—it's God's plan, not yours. He sent us to the golf course where we needed to be that day. It also illustrates the fact that we can fulfill God's plan by initiating conversations with strangers. I know that I could go to the caddy's funeral with the assurance that I shared spiritual information with him that could have led him to salvation, but God's plan was to reach his boss. I was glad I had taken the initiative to share the gospel with someone I hardly knew.

How to Approach a Stranger

It is not hard to start a Kingdom conversation with a stranger. It's always good to start by introducing yourself. If you say, "Hello, my name is …," a stranger usually will give you his or her name. This can be used in any setting: at a ball game, clothing store, or school meeting. Once introduced, you can ask questions using the FORM pattern.

After talking for a short period, depending on the time you have available, tell the person something like, "I have really enjoyed our conversation and the opportunity to get to know you better. Here is my card. How could I best get in touch with you?"

Offering him your business card first lets him know you are sincere about talking with him more. If he does not give you his card in return, you know the Holy Spirit has not called you to witness to that individual. I would then say, "If you want to talk again, give me a call."

You could also ask, "Do you have an e-mail address?" Then give him yours and ask him to send you an e-mail. If he does, you will be able to keep in touch with him. If he does not send you an e-mail, you know the Holy Spirit is not calling you to witness to that person at that time.

If the person lives in your community and you are at a little league ball game or a high school activity, you might feel comfortable saying, "Do you attend church in this area?" If he does not have a regular church, you may want to invite him to your church by saying: "You owe it to yourself to come one Sunday to (insert the name of your church)."

You can also ask him a question about a special event at your church. I use, "Have you ever heard of the Living Christmas Tree?"

This is a pageant that our church performs twelve times each Christmas season to more than 30,000 people. Many people, even if they are new to the community, have heard of the live camels and donkeys that come into the church building carrying actors who represent Jesus, Mary, or the Wise Men. I tell him I will try to find somebody who has tickets, and then explain that his children will be awestruck. I tell him if I can't find any tickets, I will put his name on the mailing list for next year's performance.

Remember, as you talk:

- Be authentic
- Be sincere
- Listen intently
- Show true interest.

If the opportunity presents itself, you may want to bring up the reason you and your family attend your church. You may also have opportunity to tell him what Christ has done for you and your family. Be sensitive to the Holy Spirit. When you share Christ with a stranger, it is the Holy Spirit who must convict him, not your presentation.

If you do have an opportunity to share Christ with a stranger, be sure to "close the sale." Ask questions such as, "Does this information make sense to you?" "Is there any reason you would not want to accept Christ today?"

If the individual chooses not to accept Christ, you can say in response, "If someone accepts Christ I cannot take the credit because the Holy Spirit must draw him to God. If someone decides to refuse Christ, I am not going to take the blame for it, either. You can accept Christ here, or when you are driving to the office, at home or in bed tonight. Either way, God gets the credit or the blame—not me!"

Then follow up with this, "But I want to tell you something you cannot do. When you get to heaven and God says, 'Why should I let you in?' you cannot say 'No one ever told me,' because I have told you. Are you sure you are still comfortable with your answer not to pray at this time?"

As you share, remember these three things:
You are God's messenger with God's message.
You may be the only Bible that person will ever see.
You need to act *now*!

Restaurant Witnessing

A very effective witnessing tool when ordering food at a restaurant can be used just after the waitress has brought your food. She will usually say, "Is there anything else I could get for you?" At that point, it is easy to say, "We are about to give thanks for our food. Is there anything we could pray about for you?"

Most waiters or waitresses will appreciate your request and will give you one or two items of concern. You may get an opportunity to tell him or her about Christ after eating, or you may discover he or she will recognize you immediately when you return to the restaurant in the future. Make sure you give a good tip for the service—you have only one chance to leave a good first impression. I have often found that when I return to a restaurant, the server I have previously prayed for will seek me out to tell me how much she appreciated my concern or will say, "Your prayer helped."

Zig Ziglar's Approach

When I asked Zig to tell me how he starts spiritual conversations, he told me that he starts many spiritual conversations simply by wearing his Fish and Seven pin. Zig explains that the fish was the sign of the early Christian. To signify that Christians serve the Lord seven days a week, Ziglar had the numeral seven superimposed over the fish to create the Fish and Seven pin. People inevitably ask him, "I know about the fish, but tell me about the seven." Zig told me, "That's a wide open door I always walk through with considerable pleasure."

Zig always autographs his books or programs with his signature and a verse of Scripture. He says, "Most of the time it's a salvation-related Scripture like Romans 10:9; John 14:6; Ephesians 2:8-9, or verses of that nature."

If you attend one of Zig's book-signing events, you'll hear many people ask him, "How are you, Zig?" He will reply, "I am blessed." Zig watches their faces to see whether their expression shows a slight change. Then he says, "That means that God has smiled on me today as He has every day since I met Him." Zig is being used of God in a mighty way as he allows Him to direct his every step looking for opportunities to share about Jesus.

I'm struck by a poem that illustrates beautifully how we are to be light in our world:

When Jesus looks upon my life,
What picture does He see?
Does He see His own reflection?
Or does He just see me?

Does He see His likeness,
The product of His hand,
Or just another Christian,
Who never took a stand?

Does He see a child of God,
A child that He set free,
Living life to honor Him,
Or does He just see me?

What about the other folks,
I meet along the way?
Do I show them Jesus,
To brighten up their day?

When someone looks into my eyes,
Can they truly see
That calm and gentle peace of God

That dwells inside of me?

When I reach out and shake a hand,
Is He right there in my grip?
Can they feel that strength from God
That steadies when I slip?

When folks are in my presence,
Do they know His Spirit's there?
Can they see that He's the one
Who guides me everywhere?

When other people think of me,
What is on their mind?
Do they think of Jesus Christ,
So gentle and so kind?

Other folks should see the joy,
That Christ has given me.
They should want to have it too,
Especially since it's free.

They should begin to ask me
What is it they must do;
Just how it is they go about
Getting Jesus, too.

Then I get to tell them,
This wondrous gift is free.
It only takes a humble heart,
A prayer on bended knee.

Someday when I'm face to face
With the Lord who set me free

Will He see His own reflection?
Or will He just see me?

    —Teresa Piercey-Gates (used with permission)

In the next chapter we will learn how to use a specially-designed tool, the *Mayishare* brochure, to witness effectively.

CHAPTER 6

How to Use the *Mayishare* Brochure

When I accepted Christ as my Savior, I knew I had found the truth. I shared my newfound faith with my three best friends. I took each of them to lunch or breakfast and said, "Listen, *sinner*, I know you are a sinner because we have done it together. You need Jesus Christ as your personal Savior." Of course, I just drove a wedge between my friends and me.

I wish I could tell you that I became more sensitive when they rejected me. I did not. I kept sharing with patients, with other dentists, or with anyone I could engage in conversation.

During the seven years I was being discipled by Pastor John Willett, he became convinced that we needed to develop a technique that would be non-threatening so that the effort I was making would see more success. He had observed, and had heard from other Christians, that I was like a bull in a china shop. I left little room for the participant to become involved in the experience because I wanted to force my point. I simply shared Christ, told the individual he or she needed Christ, and gave an invitation to pray to accept Christ. If the person did not pray to accept Christ, I was off to the next person whom I thought needed Christ *now!*

How the *Mayishare* Brochure Came to Be

John and I worked on a technique, using the back of a restaurant placemat. As I folded the placemat and asked specific questions, the individual could respond, watching as I drew diagrams and inserted Scripture. Many, many people came to know the Lord using this method which was non-threatening, but technique-sensitive. It required memorizing six scriptures and having them ready at a moment's notice.

I taught witnessing to hundreds of people, showing them how to fold the paper, insert the memorized verses and present the Gospel in a non-threatening manner. People wanting to learn how to share their faith would attend a 90-minute course I taught each week. Almost always everyone in the class would have an opportunity to share Christ by using the technique they learned during the six-week course.

However, I became discouraged because I found that if people did not use the technique for a few weeks, they would forget the verses. Forgetting the exact wording was enough to cripple them from using the method.

When I would see someone who had taken my class walking down the church hallway, I would ask if he or she had shared the gospel yet with a person I knew was on their prayer list. The answer usually was, "I'm fixing to get ready to commence to start to call them to share the Gospel."

Finally I explained to my pastor that I was not going to teach very much in the future. I would rather spend my time doing personal witnessing instead of teaching others who would not use the technique because it was easy to forget the memorized scripture.

I then asked Chad Wilt and Robert Jorgensen, who were very adept with computer skills, to help me devise a single sheet of paper that could be folded, using only three verses, and allow for interaction with the participant. After we found the pictures and wording that I thought would work, I took the brochure to several pastors and elders I respected, plus other godly people, asking for their suggestions. The brochure is now available as a free download at *www.mayishare.com*. Brochures in lots of fifty can also be ordered by contacting the publisher at *www.bmhbooks.com* or from me, Duke Heller, at 145 Green Meadows Drive, Lewis Center, Ohio, 43035; 614-888-4830. The e-mail address is *yes@mayishare.com*. A training video is also available showing the use of the brochure in a restaurant setting.

Using the *Mayishare* Brochure

After leading someone into a spiritual conversation, our goal is to get the conversation to the point that we can ask, "May I share

something with you that someone once shared with me that made it easier for me to understand God?"

Once you have received permission, show the person the front of the bro-chure.

Open the bro-chure and point to the top of the next panel. Keeping the conversation in third-party language, say, "My friend asked me this question." Read the text in the purple box.

Then say, "As a matter of fact, let me ask you the same question: 'When you die and go to heaven and God says, "(use the person's name), why should I let you in?" what are you going to say?'"

Whatever the person says is fine. This

is not an educational question; it is an informational question.

Next, point to the other box on the page.

Say, "My friend then said to me, 'Do you know it is not entirely your fault that you're a sinner?' I said, 'I know when I tell a lie, or when I steal or cheat.' My friend said, 'No, it is not entirely your fault that you are a sinner.' I then asked, 'Whose fault is it, then?' To which my friend said, 'Your parents!' I said, 'My parents?'"

Open the brochure's right panel exposing the two panels with man's attempt to build bridges to God.

Ask the person to draw two stick people beside the word *man*. Explain the story of Adam and Eve and that when they ate of the

fruit they both disobeyed God because He told them not to eat the fruit.

Ask, "When Adam and Eve ate the fruit and disobeyed God, what would we call that? The person usually will say, "sin."

Ask the person to write the word *sin* in the box under the word *man*.

Then ask him to draw two smaller stick people under Adam and Eve. Say, "The reason your children (if you have children) are sinners, is that you and your spouse are sinners and you passed this dreaded disease called 'inherent sin' to them."

Then ask them to write the word "holy" in the box underneath the word "God." God, who is holy, cannot associate with man, who is now sinful. There is a great separation between God and man.

Repeat the title line, saying, "Man has attempted to build bridges to God ever since."

Point to the top word, *baptism,* saying, "Some people say being baptized is one of those bridges. Some may be sprinkled after birth while others say you must be triple-dipped as an adult."

Point to the next word, *communion.* "Some people say taking communion once a month is sufficient while others say once per week is necessary."

Point to the next word, *church membership.* "Some people say that being a member of a certain church is their ticket to heaven."

Next ask them, "What other things can you think of that man does to find favor with God and to get to heaven?" Most people will say, "Good works." Ask the person to write down his or her answer in the blank square.

Next say, "In this illustration of man building bridges to God, if those bridges fall short and can't reach heaven, where do you think a person falls?" Most will readily say, "Hell." Have the person write *hell* in the box at the bottom of the bridge illustration. Ask, "What do you think *hell* is?" Whatever they say is okay. I personally liken it to total darkness, because God is light and missing from hell, thus it is dark, with gnashing of teeth.

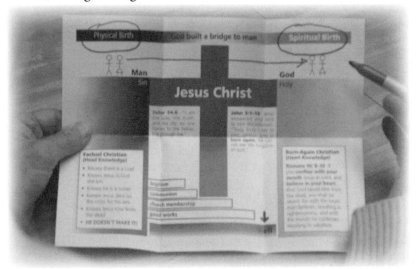

I suggest you look them in the eye at this point and say, "Hell is forever...and forever...and forever." Then open the brochure, exposing the inside page.

Now say, "God is in the bridge-building business. He built a bridge to us. That bridge is Jesus Christ." Point to the middle of the cross.

Read John 14:6, pointing to Jesus, the stick people, God, and Jesus again. Explain, "The Bible says there is only one way to get to heaven and that is through Jesus Christ."

Ask the question, "Do you know anybody who does not want to go to heaven?" Wait for a reply. Then say, "Please draw an arrow from the stick people to God. This arrow could represent you and me, you and your spouse, or it could represent Nicodemus. We find in John 3:1-10 that Nicodemus asked Jesus, 'How do I get to heaven?' Jesus answered him, 'You must be born again.' Have you heard of the term 'born again'?"

Most people have heard of the term. Point to the upper left panel portion showing *Physical Birth* and say, "Nicodemus assumed Jesus was speaking about a physical birth, when in fact Jesus was speaking of a spiritual birth." Point to the panel showing *Spiritual Birth* in the upper right panel section.

This next section is very important. Tell the person, "Just as you were born into sin from Adam and Eve, you can be born again into salvation."

Then say, "Let me explain what a 'factual Christian' is. A 'factual Christian' is someone who has head knowledge." Now point to the individual items saying, "This is someone who 'knows there is a God.'" Then proceed down the list of five items. After the last item, "Knows Jesus rose from the dead," emphasize the statement, "he doesn't make it."

Then say, "All of these facts are true. Satan believes each one of these statements. The reason this person does not make it is because there are two parts of being born again. Romans 10:9-10, states.... (Let the person read the passage on the right side of the pamphlet.)

Point out the bold words, "The first part is 'believe in your heart.' That is the facts. The second point is 'Confess with your mouth Jesus as your personal Savior.'"

Next fold the panel down on itself and turn the right panel over, exposing the picture with the wording, "Can you point to an exact time you accepted Christ as your personal Savior?"

Listen to the person's answer. If he or she has never made a commitment, or seems unsure of an exact date, say, "May I ask you two questions?"

The first question is, "Does this information make sense to you?"

Wait for a reply. Next ask, "Is there any reason you would not want to accept Jesus Christ right now?"

If you sense uncertainty, say "Let me share with you what is involved."

Turn the brochure over to green section and share what he or she must do to accept Christ.

1. Confess with your mouth you are a sinner
2. Pray and ask Jesus to forgive you of your sins
3. Ask Christ to become the Lord of your life.

You can then say, "Just as you were born into sin, you can be born into salvation."

If the person prays out loud to accept Christ, then you pray out loud thanking the Holy Spirit for drawing

him or her to God. Comment that the angels in heaven are rejoicing with the decision. Ask Jesus to become a large part of the person's life decision to make Him Lord.

If the person says he or she is not ready to accept Christ at this time, continue:

"I can understand your hesitation, but may I share something with you? You can accept Christ here today, or you can do it in your car, or you can do it at home tonight, or you can never do it. But I will tell you something you cannot do. When you get to heaven and God says, '(person's name) why should I let you in?' you can never say to God, 'Nobody ever told me,' because I have told you."

You can also add, "If you accept Christ I cannot take credit for it because the Holy Spirit must draw you. However, if you decide not to accept Christ, I am not going to take the blame. My responsibility is to share the information. It is your responsibility to act on the information—if God is calling you!"

I've been instructed and stimulated in my witnessing efforts by a concept I heard from a missionary. Read about it in the next chapter.

CHAPTER 7

Don't Wait for Them to Come

Visitors to a church and walk-ins account for only ten percent of born-again conversions, while eighty-five percent of all conversions are the result of the influence of friends or relatives. These statistics from the Institute of Church Growth (Navigators) show us that, to reach people for Christ, making friends is extremely important.

Larry DeArmey, a veteran missionary to Spain, gave a great message at our church entitled, "The Progress of the Gospel in the World," and his text was Romans 15:5-11. He shared the importance of going into the world to meet people where they are, on their terrain, because many will not come to our churches. In part of his message, he said there are two categories of people we will encounter, seekers and non-seekers, both from a human perspective and from God's. The remainder of this chapter is a summary of his material.

Non-Seekers

DeArmey pointed out that among the non-seekers there are two distinct types. There are those who are obviously not looking for answers in life.

Non-seeking Non-seekers

This is the term DeArmey uses to identify those who are too preoccupied with the cares of this life or by material gain to be seeking anything else. Realism, skepticism, and pessimism characterize their lives. Many of them are thirty and older. They are very difficult to reach and relatively few become converted. They are not seekers. They are indifferent to spiritual things and do not want to talk about them. It is evident, both to men and God, that they are not seeking spiritual food.

Seeking Non-seekers

These people are looking primarily for relationships with others, and they are willing to turn to almost anything or anyone to help fill the void. Their search is not primarily spiritual, but spirituality will draw them if it guarantees relationship with others. This group is characterized by disappointment and disillusionment. They are found in all age groups. They appear to be seeking, but are not truly seeking. They are looking for relationships and want free handouts. They have no heart-desire to encounter God. To us they may appear to be genuine seekers, but God knows they are not interested in a relationship with Jesus Christ.

Seekers

Seeking Seekers

These individuals are deeply interested in finding true meaning to their lives and are willing to consider answers coming from more traditional sources. They may seek out your church, prepared for a gospel presentation. These people are ripe for picking—like fruit falling off the tree. God has prepared their hearts for gospel truth. They are searching for God and contentment.

Idealism and disappointment characterize this group. They come from all age categories. They are few and far between, but when discovered, they provide great opportunities. They are true seekers, and they will often come to us.

Non-seeking Seekers

These people are deeply interested in finding true meaning to their lives. They are not interested, however, in traditional answers, such as those offered by religion. They turn, therefore, to non-traditional systems for answers. Many are in a clearly defined age group—young adults—and have a New Age background. They have rejected anything Christian and are not openly seeking. They do want a spiritual dimension in their lives, however, and their hearts are still seeking, although they may not be aware of it.

Non-seekers likely reject invitations to church activities. It's hard to tell whether they are true seekers after spiritual things, but they are idealists and are seeking something real although they likely cannot define what that is. Because of the apparent lack of spiritual receptivity, they often intimidate Christians. But they are true searchers, and we must seek them.

These so-called "non-seeking seekers" are people with whom we work and socialize. We're already praying for many of them. God has looked in their hearts and knows they are seeking. Prayer will bring people and circumstances into their lives that will soften their hearts toward spiritual things. Because of their present struggle, these people become strong Christians once they accept Christ. It is important for them to see God working in us.

Conclusion

Although non-seekers are not church-attenders, on occasion you might meet a visitor who has come to church at the invitation of a friend. Be sure to make the guest feel welcomed, realizing that God has brought him or her to that place at that time. Use the opportunity to make a contact with a view to developing a relationship over time if God allows.

Remember, however, that it is essential for believers to seek opportunities to meet non-believers on their turf.

Larry DeArmey, from whom most of this chapter was adapted, noted that the church is called to sing God's praises *among the nations* (Romans 15:9, paraphrase). Too often we wait for people to come in *among us*. Though some might come, most do not. It is very important, therefore, that we go out to them.

How do you deal with people who raise objections to your witness? In the next chapter, we turn our attention to some of the most common objections, and we discuss how to respond to them.

CHAPTER 8

Overcoming Objections

A dental surgeon who had been a college professor of mine became sick with cancer. He fought the disease for a few years and assumed he had beaten it. When he learned that the disease had returned, he took all of the items from his desk, put them in a cardboard box, and went home to die. He changed his telephone number and said he did not want to talk to or see anyone.

When I heard about his illness, I called his best friend, asking for the unlisted telephone number. I had to beg for the number, promising that I would not tell the professor how I got it.

I called his house. His wife answered and called him to the phone. He immediately asked how I got the telephone number and why I was calling him, since he could not refer any patients for dental implants to me.

I Don't Want to Talk about It

I assured him I was not calling for referrals, but just wanted to see how he was doing.

"Not very well, but I will be OK," he replied. Without thinking, I said, "Dr. A--, do you ever eat lunch?" After his affirmative reply, I said, "Good. Meet me at the Whaling Station Restaurant tomorrow at noon, and don't be late."

I hung up the phone before he could tell me he was not coming.

A few minutes later one of the office assistants told me there was a Dr. A on the phone and he insisted on talking to me. I told my receptionist to tell him, "Duke is not available. Be at the restaurant tomorrow, and don't be late!"

The next day he came to the restaurant but declared he was not going to stay unless I told him what I wanted to talk to him about. I told him I just wanted to say "thank you" for all of the men he had trained and all of the great teaching he had done for more than thirty-five years.

He softened, and we sat down at the table. That was at noon. We left the restaurant at 3:45 that afternoon, with tears in our eyes. It was so much fun to thank him for the positive surgical influence he had in my life and for the many men he had trained as oral surgeons.

Early in the conversation, I said, "They tell me you are really sick again."

"I don't want to talk about it," he replied.

"Yes you do," I said. "I know it is on your mind constantly. Why would you not want to talk about something that is on your mind constantly? Tell me about it."

Dr. A then began to tell me how he had fought the disease and how he was so proud of his accomplishments in teaching. He named many men he had trained and the joy he felt over their success. He allowed me to ask questions about his family, his career, or his health, but he would not allow me to talk about spiritual matters. I tried to start the conversation several times, but he would always shut me down. At that time in my own spiritual growth of sharing Christ, I allowed his resistance or sickness to keep me from pursuing the topic.

For several days following his death I felt sick because, to my knowledge, he died without making a commitment to Christ. I could look in his casket knowing I had attempted to share Christ with him. I believe that today, however, with my experience in handling objections, I could have more easily transitioned into the Bridge illustration. I would have asked him, "When you do die in the near future and get to heaven and God asks 'Why should I let you in?' what are you going to say?"

Most of us would agree that one of the main reasons we do not share our faith is because of fear. We are afraid of what people are going to say. We are afraid of what they are going to think. We are afraid of how it will affect our relationship with them.

F.E.A.R.

Zig Ziglar has a great acronym: F.E.A.R. – *False Evidence Appearing Real.* Satan wants us to believe that we cannot talk about religion. Nothing could be farther from the truth. We talk about politics, another tough topic, almost every day. We can also easily talk about religion every day if we choose our words properly, mostly by asking pointed questions.

But many people put off talking about their beliefs because of this fear: "What if they bring up an objection I can't answer? What will I say?"

Even though people can quote the verse, "[G]reater is He who is in you than he who is in the world" (1 John 4:4), they still want to have answers to handle objections. Very seldom do these objections surface when presenting the Gospel. However, I find people are more comfortable if they are ready with information or answers to counter objections.

Please try to remember that many questions unbelievers ask are designed to take you down a rabbit trail; they are an attempt to keep you from revealing the truth. Be sure you don't make fun of anyone whose statement or question seems ridiculous. God can use the question to help that person find the truth.

A Helpful Suggestion

In the next chapter I will discuss answers to specific objections, but first allow me to give you a technique that works well in overcoming objections. If someone asks me a question, I repeat the question directly back to him. When you repeat the question, you are hitting the conversation tennis ball back into his court.

Here is an example.

Let's assume the person says, "Is Christ the only way to God?" Look him in the eye and repeat, "Is Christ the *only* way to God?" Emphasize the word "only." I would then be silent. The conversation ball is now in his court. Since silence between two people is difficult to tolerate, the person will usually respond with something like: "Yes, you told me that the Bible said God was the only way to heaven. What about the Jews, the Muslims, or atheists? Don't you think all religious roads lead to heaven?"

I would repeat, "All roads lead to heaven?" Then I would stay quiet and listen for his reply. Usually he will say, "I have heard that all religions are similar" or "Don't all religions have the same God? They just use different pathways to get to God."

I would then ask, "Do you believe all religions have the same God?"

Listen for his answer. Then say, "The Bible says that not all roads are the same. The God of the Bible is not the same God as the Muslim God. The Bible says that Jesus Christ is the only way to the one true God."

Try to bring the conversation back to helping the person realize he has a personal accountability to Jesus Christ. Be very specific and say, "The Bible says that Christ is the only way to heaven. It is not what [insert your name] thinks. Only what God says is important."

Only One Way

I often quote what Jesus says to His disciple Thomas in John 14: 6: "I am the way, and the truth, and the life; no one comes to the Father, but through Me."

Christians are not being prejudiced or presumptuous when they say that Jesus Christ is the only way to God and heaven. As Christians, we have no other option, because Christ Himself made this statement to Thomas, and John recorded His words.

Although one may choose to believe whatever he wishes, he has no right to redefine Christianity in his own terms. If the person feels there must be more than one way to heaven, I would ask him, "How do you handle guilt when you sin? What is your plan for salvation?" Listen without interruption, looking him in the eyes. Allow a few seconds of silence. Then simply ask, "Why is your opinion more reasonable than the Bible?"

Many times the person will admit it is only a personal opinion but insist that he is entitled to his opinion, as the Jews or Muslims are entitled to their opinion. I will then tell him, "But this is not my opinion. This is the Bible's opinion. I would be afraid to use my opinion to defend what God will or will not do when He sees me after I die."

I sometimes will tell a story to illustrate a point about judgment and law. I use the example of driving a car down the highway at 60 mph in a 45 mph zone. If a police officer pulls me over and presents me with a radar report, I am in trouble. I may think I had the right to go faster because there was nobody else on the road, I was passing a slower car, or I was late to pick up my stranded child at school. However, the law says I am guilty. My opinion is not important. The law is the law. Even if I appeal and a lenient judge waives or reduces the fine, I am still guilty. God is a judge who is judging *life*—in heaven or in hell! What if He goes strictly by the law? Am I guilty?

Keep in mind that people often ask questions to take the attention off themselves. I want to guide the conversation back to them and to their relationship with Jesus Christ. I do this by asking, "Do you feel you can point to an exact time that you made a commitment to Christ? Tell me about it." This question will get them off other religious highways and direct the conversation back to them—where it started.

Reading Scripture

A few, selected Scripture verses are very powerful. Use them. If possible, turn the Bible so your friend can also read the Scripture with you. I always pray, asking God to work through His written

Scripture in the heart of the individual who is reading the Scripture with me. God's Word is sharper than any two-edged sword (Hebrews 4:12); your words of wisdom may only dull God's sword! We can never go wrong by quoting the Bible and letting Scripture verses speak for us, defining why we believe what we believe.

Guard against using too much Scripture, though. Most people will be uneasy reading Scripture since they are unfamiliar with the Bible. A little Scripture used wisely will not overload their brains. Furthermore, it is up to the Holy Spirit to convict them, and the Holy Spirit can use your weak words as well as God's Holy Word.

Making the Appeal

Assuming that the Holy Spirit enabled me to answer their questions and concerns, I like to use positive statements, anticipating a favorable decision for Christ. For example, "Bill, when you make a commitment to Christ, you will discover what it means to have real peace, peace with God!" Or, "When you accept Christ, you will find that the Bible will make more sense to you, because you will have the Author in your heart."

When talking with a successful businessman, I often use a poem of Blaise Pascal. Pascal was a French mathematician and philosopher who said that "man is born with a God-shaped vacuum."

Filling the Vacuum

Pascal wrote:

There once was in man a true happiness of which now remain to him only the mark and empty trace, which he in vain tries to fill from all his surroundings, seeking from things absent the help he does not obtain in things present. But these are all inadequate, because the infinite abyss can only be filled by an infinite and immutable object, that is to say, only by God Himself. (Blaise Pascal, *Pascal's Pensees*, translated by W. F. Trotter [New York: E.P. Dutton, 1958], 113

Man will try to fill that vacuum with sex, money, fame, or reputation, but he will remain unfulfilled because he has a God-shaped vacuum. I usually will add, "When you accept Christ, Bill, you will lose that empty feeling and fill it with God's formula for success *if* you sell out to Christ one hundred percent. You have been trying it your way for many years. Are you really where you want to be in your relationship with God? Do you feel the Holy Spirit is calling you to make a commitment to Christ at this time?"

If you don't ask for the sale you will not get it. If the Holy Spirit is calling the person, he or she is ready to pray. If the Holy Spirit is not calling them, the person is not ready to pray. The Holy Spirit has called you to be the vehicle to deliver the information. The decision is up to the individual and the power of the Holy Spirit.

What if the individual does not accept Christ? Realize that the Holy Spirit is not calling the person at this time. You can't fail personally, no matter what someone does with the invitation to accept Christ as Savior.

Now let's move into discussing how to deal with some specific objections to accepting Christ.

CHAPTER 9

Responding to Common Objections

Here are some common objections and examples of how to respond effectively:

Why Did God Allow My Mother To Die?

I would repeat the question because I don't know exactly what they are asking me. I would say, "Why did God allow your mother to die?"

"Yes. You told me that God allows everything that happens. So why would a loving God allow my mother to die?" My reply would then be, "I think a better question might be, 'Why did your mother die?' Why do you think your mother died?" Usually they will give you an answer such as she had cancer or was in an accident.

I would then tell about Adam and Eve, explaining that they had great fellowship with God after they were created. God put them in charge of the animal kingdom and told them they were in total control. If they told the fish to jump out of the water, the fish would obey. If they told the lion to lie down with the lamb, the lion would do it. However, God did tell Adam and Eve they could not eat from one tree. If they did, they would die. They disobeyed God and ate from that tree.

Then I would ask, "What would we call disobeying God?" Almost everyone will reply, "Sin." I then tell them that sin was passed on from Adam and Eve to us through our parents. "The reason my son is a sinner is that Wanda and I are sinners." I then look directly in their eyes saying, "The reason you are a sinner is because your parents are sinners."

Then I explain, "Cancer or an accident did not kill your mother. It was sin that killed your mother." My answer is based on the clear teaching of the Bible that the reason men are sinners is that our parents—all the way back to Adam and Eve—were sinners. The ultimate cause of a mother's death—though perhaps not the immediate cause—is sin. I then ask this simple question. "You're going to die someday, aren't you?" Everyone will reply, "Yes." "It was sin that killed your mother, not God; and sin will also be responsible for killing you."

Be sensitive to the hurt a recent death of a loved one may be causing in the life of the individual you are attempting to reach for Christ.

Why Do the Innocent Suffer?
Why Are Some Babies Born with Defects?
Why Are Wars Allowed?

The Bible clearly tells us that when God created the universe it was perfect. Man was given the freedom to obey God or disobey Him; it was man's choice. Evil came into the universe through man's disobedience and Satan's influence. Ultimately, sickness and suffering are the result of sin. Evil entered into human experience because of Adam's disobedience in the very first confrontation with temptation.

This answer will many times elicit another question: Why doesn't God do away with evil and sickness?

I usually repeat the question word-for-word and immediately say, "If all evil were stamped out of the universe tonight at midnight—

which one of us would be here at one o'clock in the morning?" I know I personally have enough sin and evil in my life to be labeled "guilty"!

If time allows, I would tell them that God does not permit innocent babies to suffer for His sake. I would take the person to John 9:1-3: "And as He passed by, He saw a man blind from birth. And His disciples asked Him, saying, 'Rabbi, who sinned, this man or his parents, that he should be born blind?' Jesus answered, 'It was neither that this man sinned, nor his parents; but it was in order that the works of God might be displayed in him.'"

This is always a good Scripture to read concerning those born with defects. The Scripture clearly shows that though sin is the ultimate cause of all disease, deformity, and death, it was not the immediate cause of this man's blindness. God will use the man's blindness for His glory in the lives of many people—to draw those people unto Himself.

Do You Honestly Believe Jesus Christ Is God?

Many times in helping a non-Christian think through the intellectual aspect of Christianity, our best defense is a good offense. I like to ask this question with an explanation: "Which of the four possible conclusions about Jesus Christ and His claims do you accept?"

1. He was a Liar. Even those who deny His deity will invariably hasten to assure us that Jesus was a great moral philosopher and teacher, not a liar.

2. He was a Lunatic. This conclusion would not destroy His moral integrity.

3. He was a Legend. Legends are man-made. Were Richard Nixon or Abraham Lincoln legends? If they claimed to be God, would you have believed them if they said that they could forgive sins, and then rose from the dead? The Bible and Jewish historians clearly tell us that five hundred people saw Jesus in a resurrected state of being.

4. He was Truth. What He did and said is recorded in the Bible and it is all true—every word and deed.

If the listener concedes tht none of the first three are satisfactory answers, point out that number four is the only logical conclusion. Give him an opportunity to think through that issue before proceeding with your presentation.

Can You Prove Scientifically that God Exists?

I would reply by repeating the question and asking another question: "Can I prove scientifically that God exists? Can you prove He doesn't?"

Scientists might bring this up because they want to be able to prove all existence with valid experiments. We must remember that the scientific method is limited to measurable aspects of reality. Can you measure love? Yet you know it exists! Can you measure fear? Yet you know it exists! You do not need to prove love scientifically to know that it exists and to enjoy the benefits and truths of love.

Point out that man cannot explain how the Egyptians built the pyramids, yet we know they exist. There are two theories: The first is that a large hole was dug, 300-500 foot deep, and the building materials were lowered into the hole. The pyramid was built and the dirt was taken away, leaving level ground around the existing pyramids. This reasoning, of course, would have to account for movement of hundreds of tons of dirt since level ground surrounds the pyramids today.

The other theory is that the foundation was laid with rocks of various shapes, each weighing many tons. As the height of the pyramid increased, additional dirt would be brought in and packed down, allowing large stones to be rolled on large wooden poles and placed in triangular fashion—fitting so closely that you cannot get a credit card between the surfaces of the rocks. You can ask, "Since scientists cannot prove how the pyramids were built, do you think they doubt their existence?"

I also like to point out that man can watch billions of gallons of water flow into the ocean, yet the ocean does not overflow. Scientists can prove that evaporation cannot possibly remove enough excess water to keep the oceans constant and level.

If I Could See God, I Could Believe in Him.

I usually have two replies when they state why they want to be able to see God. The first is, "Have you ever seen electricity? You have seen the effects of electricity but you have never seen electricity; still, you know that it exists because you can see the effects of its power." Immediately follow that statement by asking, "Why do you need to see God to know that He exists?"

I Don't Believe in a Heaven and Hell. I Think We Just Turn into Dust at Death.

You may want to tell them, "The Bible tells a story about a rich man and a poor man who both died. The rich man did not believe in hell but found himself there after death."

You can read them the story of Lazarus and the rich man in Luke 16: 19-31. On earth, Lazarus had been the rich man's slave. After they died, Lazarus was in Abraham's bosom (heaven) and the rich man was in hades (hell). The rich man begged Abraham to send someone to warn his brothers about the horrors of hades.

After reading the verses, say, "If I died, and you came to my funeral and watched me being lowered in the ground, would you believe I was dead? If I knocked on your door a year later and said, '[Bill], God has sent me to tell you that you need to accept Christ right now or go to hell forever,' would you believe it was me?"

Will the Person Who Has Never Heard of Jesus Be Condemned to Hell?

We must admit that we don't know how God will deal with these people, but we want to bring up the following points that can be supported with Scripture.

God is just. We can have confidence in His character. We can trust that God will be fair to those who have never heard of Jesus Christ.

No person will be condemned for rejecting Jesus Christ of whom he has never heard; instead, he will be condemned for violating his own moral standard. You can read Romans 2:11-16 to them.

Scripture indicates in Romans 1:19-20, 25 that every man has enough information from creation to know that God exists.

There is no indication in the Bible that a man can be saved apart from Jesus Christ. We can hang our hat on John 14:6, which states that Jesus is the way and the truth and the life; no one gets to the Father except through Him.

Aren't There Errors in the Bible?

Repeat the question, "Do you think the Bible is full of errors?" Then add, "Do you know of any errors?" They may have heard someone else say that the Bible was full of errors or contradictions and they have believed those assumptions. Usually if you remain silent after repeating their question back to them, they will become confused because they have no particular verse in mind.

If they do bring up a question about a certain Scripture or a specific situation that you cannot accurately answer, listen carefully. Write down their question, saying, "That is a good question. I do not know the answer, but I will get the answer for you. Let me make sure I have written your question down correctly. Can I get back with you in a couple of days?" You do not have to have all of the answers. It is better to get the correct answer later than to try to bluff your way through an answer.

Dr. Nelson Glueck, a Jewish archaeologist, made this remarkable statement: "No archaeological discovery has ever controverted a Biblical reference. Scores of archaeological findings have been made which confirm in clear outline or in exact detail historical statements in the Bible. And, by the same token, proper evaluation of Biblical descriptions has often led to amazing discoveries." (Nelson Glueck, *Rivers in the Desert.* New York: Farrar, Strauss and Cudahy, 1959, p. 31). We cannot waver in our belief that every word of the Bible is true and inspired by God through men.

I Learned in College That Evolution Is How Humans Got Here.

It is not very wise to get in a spitting contest with someone who has learned a lot of false information about humans coming from two cells and dividing into male and female humans after "Big Foot." Evolution is not the issue, but you may have to address it, so perhaps the following questions can help.

"What conclusions are you drawing from your evolutionary position? Are you saying the universe happened by chance? Or are you saying that God created the universe and did so by using certain evolutionary processes?"

Most people do not have enough scientific knowledge to argue a position of evolution versus creationism. Many books can answer their questions better than we can. Many websites can also help them learn more quickly by addressing these kinds of questions. Excellent resources are available at *www.answers.org* and *www.answersingenesis.org*.

I Think God Will Grade on the Curve. If We Lead a Good, Moral Life, He Will Let Us Into Heaven!

This kind of thinking shows incredible optimism about man's righteousness and an unbelievable ignorance of God's infinite Holiness. God is not going to grade on the curve. There are no A's, B's, or C's in God's grading system. There is only truth—black versus white.

I will sometimes say, "Do you think some sins are worse than others? Do you think stealing a dime is as bad as killing someone?" Most people rate or prioritize crimes; however, a sin is a sin. When someone answers yes to the previous question, I then ask him, "Why do you think God would prioritize sin?"

Another technique that works well is to ask the person, "Where do morals come from?" He may say he learned moral character from his parents or from a school teacher. When you ask him, "Where did your parents and grandparents and their grandparents learn morals?" eventually he should arrive at the Ten Commandments.

There Are Too Many Hypocrites in the Church!

To this comeback, try replying, "Have you ever seen a counterfeit twenty-dollar bill?" It is tough to detect the counterfeit from the real thing. The reason you see counterfeit Christians is that the real Christian is worth counterfeiting. Counterfeit Christians are attempting in a worldly, secular, sinful way to imitate something they know to be good. By saying there are hypocrites in the church, they are really paying the church a very high compliment. I usually make fun of myself by saying, "When I brought that objection up to one of my Christian friends, he replied to me, 'Duke, please come to our church, as one more hypocrite won't make any difference.'" This usually gets a little laugh, plus they have probably heard the analogy used before.

You do not have to be able to answer everyone's questions and objections in order to be an effective witness for Christ. After all, there is a lot that we don't know; only God has all the answers. However, the Holy Spirit will aid you in responding to legitimate questions.

Don't be afraid to admit that you don't have an answer. But we must accept at face value what the Bible says. It is God's Word and it is clear enough about His plan of salvation that anyone who rejects the truth is without excuse.

In the next several chapters we will look at the use of the Ten Commandments, which can be particularly effective with certain people.

Chapter 10

Why the Law Still Works

After reading Ray Comfort's book, *Hell's Best Kept Secret*, I revisited my thinking and realized that the Law (the Ten Commandments) can and should be an important part of witnessing. Many of the ideas for this chapter come from that book. Comfort says, "the preaching of the Law is hell's best-kept secret."

Discussing the Ten Commandments is one of the best ways to produce conviction in the heart of a non-Christian. I also use the Ten Commandments when witnessing to Muslims or Jews, as they are grounded in Abrahamic history and they often feel held accountable for God's rules found in Exodus 20:1-17.

Discussion of the ten basics of spiritual and moral law, when viewed from God's point of view, is very sobering to the sinner who, in a time of uncertainty, is honestly looking to find God. The Law cuts the self-righteous down to size quickly as they realize that even with Christ offering grace to us, we fall very short of keeping the Ten Commandments.

Here are the commandments and some points to consider as you discuss them with the person to whom you are witnessing.

1. You Shall Have No Other Gods Before Me.

This is number one on the list, which means that God places great importance on it. We should love God with all of our heart, with all of our soul and mind, and with all of our strength (Mark 12: 30). I fail this first law more often than I want to admit. Our love for the Creator should be so great that all other affections take a back seat in comparison.

Jesus said in Luke 14:26, "If anyone comes to Me, and does not hate his own father and mother and wife and children and brothers and sisters, yes, and even his own life, he cannot be My disciple." That certainly makes it clear that my own wife and children, whom I hold as most important in my human existence, must come after Christ. Christians must be mature to accept the order of these relationships because we pride ourselves on how important families are to the Christian. It is easy to say you love God more than money, but it is a different thing to live like God is more important than your children, your grandchildren, or your spouse. But God said it, so it is true.

2. You Shall Not Make for Yourself an Idol.

Most Christians can easily accept the fact that 100-foot-tall Buddhist carvings are useless. It is much more difficult to accept Christ as He is, instead of how we want Him to be. Many new converts to the Christian faith want to add Jesus to their lives. They want to add Christ to their bowling league, to their overloaded work schedule, to their Little League schedule, and to other areas of their life. Christ must take the place of prominence in our schedule, our thought life, and in our prayer life to help us overcome the disappointments of life.

> For even though they knew God, they did not honor Him as God, or give thanks, but they became futile in their speculations, and their foolish heart was darkened. Professing to be wise, they became fools, and exchanged the glory of the incorruptible God for an image in the form of corruptible man and of birds and four-footed animals and crawling creatures. Therefore God gave them over in the lusts of their hearts to impurity, that

their bodies might be dishonored among them. For they exchanged the truth of God for a lie, and worshiped and served the creature rather than the Creator, who is blessed forever. Amen (Romans 1:21-25).

Many people today want to make their God "love." The word love is thrown around as a magical term that attracts people who want to sound spiritual. Who can argue with love? God can. Many people make God into their own image of love as a covering for not looking at their own sin. Most of these people do not want to accept the fact that a loving God would make a hell where love could not be present. The truth is, it does not matter what people believe about God. God tells us in Malachi 3:6, "For I, the Lord, do not change; therefore you, O sons of Jacob, are not consumed."

3. You Shall Not Take the Name of the Lord Your God in Vain.

Whatever comes out of your mouth that is distasteful to God really does matter. Jesus said in Matthew 12:36, "...I say to you that every careless word that men shall speak, they shall render account for it in the day of judgment."

Before becoming a Christian, I used to "cuss," assuming that my words of wisdom, when mixed with swear words, could make a bigger impact with my audience. I used to sit in audiences, hear other speakers swear to make a point, and criticize them silently. Still I continued to do the same thing.

After I accepted Christ as personal Savior, my words became more important to me. I realized that swearing was in fact "blaspheming" the Lord God. I learned that when I took the name of God, the Holy Name of my Creator and Savior, and brought it down to the level of filth, God could not bless my life. At least He could not bless my conversation with others. This third commandment is overlooked in today's society because people do not take it seriously. God, of course, must feel differently because He made it number three on His list.

4. Remember the Sabbath Day, to Keep it Holy.

God took six days to create His world and on the seventh day He rested (Genesis 2:2). Old Testament saints used the seventh day to rest and worship God. New Testament saints began to observe Sunday (the Lord's Day) to celebrate Christ's resurrection (Acts 20: 7; 1 Corinthians 16:2).

Today, however, busy Americans seem not to be able to find a "Sabbath day" for rest in their week. Many Christians have traditionally considered Sunday not only as a day for corporate worship, but also as a day for rest. That tradition is rapidly disappearing, however, with sporting events of all kinds and other activities demanding both Saturday and Sunday involvements for many enthusiasts, whether athletes or fans.

How should New Testament Christians regard God's command about the Sabbath? The underlying principle seems clear--a day of rest is essential for human beings to maintain their physical, emotional, and mental well-being. We need both a time to worship God and a time to rest. God wants us to be quiet so His Word can penetrate our lives. Times of rest will restore and refresh our physical being. And times of worship on Sunday will give believers a fragrant smell of God's presence in their lives throughout the week at home, at work, and within their own hearts and minds.

5. Honor Your Father and Mother.

If we are going to honor or value our parents, we will need to embrace this concept. Since many young people feel their parents exist to serve them, they don't need to obey their "old man." Looking back on my teenage years and the disrespectful way I treated my parents, I see that my actions would have been enough to send me to hades, if honoring my parents was the only commandment. As with most teenagers, my goals in life were playing sports and gaining whatever life could give me—not honoring my parents.

After I became a Christian, I realized that I needed to teach this commandment to my children so they (and I) could better serve God. God thought enough of honoring parents that He made it fifth on the list—ahead of murder and stealing.

Ephesians 6:1-4 clearly declares, "Children, obey your parents in the Lord, for this is right. Honor your father and mother (which is the first commandment with a promise), that it may be well with you, and that you may live long on the earth. And, fathers, do not provoke your children to anger; but bring them up in the discipline and instruction of the Lord."

Our review of the Ten Commandments continues with the second half in the next chapter.

CHAPTER 11

More on the Law

The Law not only makes sinners tremble, it also makes them realize they do not measure up to God's standards. It is difficult for me to understand how saved or unsaved people can enjoy the pleasures of sin, knowing that the eye of a holy God is viewing their every move, word, and deed.

If you decide to use the Ten Commandments to bring someone to a saving knowledge of grace, do not sugarcoat Scripture. Here are some points about the final five commandments.

6. You Shall Not Murder

Old Testament saints were aware of this commandment guiding their relationships with their fellowman. The New Testament tells us that our thoughts, also, can kill. Jesus raised the standard.

1 John 3:15 warns, "Everyone who hates his brother is a murderer; and you know that no murderer has eternal life abiding in him." This certainly sheds a different light on our inward thoughts. Most of us have had people in our lives who, for various reasons, we truly hated. Often it was because the person caused us or a member of our family a great deal of pain or discomfort.

Matthew 5:21-22 takes it to a different level when Jesus says, "You have heard that the ancients were told, 'You shall not commit murder' and 'Whoever commits murder shall be liable to the court.'

But I say to you that everyone who is angry with his brother shall be guilty before the court; and whoever shall say to his brother, 'Raca' (or 'You good-for-nothing'), shall be guilty before the supreme court; and whoever says 'You fool,' shall be guilty enough to go into the fiery hell."

It seems clear that Jesus has put a new definition on the word *murder* and how we will be held accountable. Hating a person who has harmed me, being angry with him for his actions against me or a member of my family, or calling him a derogatory name puts me in danger of hell's fire, just as if I had put a gun to the one who offended me by his words or actions. Who has avoided the guilt of this commandment?

7. You Shall Not Commit Adultery

The Old Testament sentences to death by stoning a person who is guilty of adultery. The New Testament takes the definition of adultery to an even higher level. Jesus tells us in Matthew 5:28, "[B]ut I say to you that everyone who looks on a woman with lust for her has already committed adultery with her in his heart."

Every man who ever lived, except Jesus, is guilty of lust from his teenage years to old age. Before becoming a Christian, I used to tell my daughters that every man is an animal. I cautioned them not to believe the sweet-talking kind or those promising bliss—because they have only sex on their minds. Of course, I was using myself as an example.

After becoming a Christian I wanted desperately not to look at other women with lust. The harder I tried, the harder it became. Satan can easily get into the heart and mind of a good Christian leader and destroy his ministry by ruining his thought life. Every man reading this book struggles with lust, and he lusts with his eyes.

Steven Arterburn and Fred Stoeker wrote a book, *Every Man's Battle,* which teaches Christian men how to win the war on sexual temptation. All pastors and lay leaders need to read and outline this book to help themselves or those who come to them wanting to be mentored for spiritual growth. This struggle against lust can be won, one victory at a time, until it is under control. George Barna of The Barna Group (*www.barna.org*) reports that many pastors deal with the problem of pornography in their lives. Certainly the problem starts with the eyes.

Adultery is accepted today as natural, and there is a fifty-percent divorce rate among adults. Kids, male and female, grow up with a media blitz that tells them sex is the way to get that certain person who can satisfy all of their needs. Women are depicted as objects of passion to serve the sexual desires of males. Rape occurs daily in many high schools because boys are exposed to their fathers' *Playboy* magazines or web pornography. God is very clear. What we think about is important enough that God will hold us accountable.

8. You Shall Not Steal

In early childhood, most of us find that we have a desire for another child's toys. If those toys happen to end up in our toy box, we are pleased. What do you have to steal to be a thief? A paper clip from the office? A pencil from school? What about cheating on our taxes, using the excuse that the government does not use our money wisely anyway? Without the blood of Jesus, the unsaved person will be guilty before God with a punishment of eternal hell for stealing.

Both the Old and New Testaments describe not only sins of commission but sins of omission, as well. If we have the ability to help someone with our resources or time, but fail to do it, we are just as guilty as if we stole from him. James 4:17 says, "Therefore, to one who knows the right thing to do and does not do it, to him it is sin."

Proverbs 3:27-28 instructs us, "Do not withhold good from those to whom it is due, when it is in your power to do it. Do not say to your neighbor, 'Go, and come back, and tomorrow I will give it,' when you have it with you."

Sometimes we are all selfish with our time and resources. Most of us don't think about our wrong use of time as a sin against God.

Looking at a man's checkbook will tell you where his heart is, as well as his values. Christians realize that the first ten percent of their paycheck should be given to God, so He can bless the use of the remaining ninety percent. Since all one hundred percent is His, we should be thankful to have control of the ninety percent. Whether the ten percent is before or after taxes is a personal decision that must be bathed in prayer.

Many of us view giving our tithes and offerings as being more important than giving our time to the church. If we are going to tithe ten percent of our money, why don't we also tithe ten percent of our time to the church?

The talents God has given the Christian can be compared to money in the bank. If we are mediocre Christians at using our talents, God will find it difficult to use us. How do you compare to those people who work very hard to do their best in your workplace? We are God's representatives in our workplaces and must realize that we may be the only "Jesus" our coworkers will ever see. Nothing is more sickening to the Christian than to see sloppy, under-achieving, over-critical, under-disciplined, mediocre people claiming that Christ is the most important thing in their lives. The outside world sees through our spiritual balloon as we steal from our potential and from God's expectations for us.

9. You Shall Not Bear False Witness Against Your Neighbor

Satan told Eve the very first lie when he said that if she ate of the forbidden fruit, "You surely shall not die" (Gen. 3:4). Some of us feel there are degrees of telling fibs or "white lies."

It is easy to identify with calling our neighbor an "idiot" for chopping down our tree by mistake, compared to remaining silent when a different neighbor tells an untruth about the same neighbor who chopped down our tree. Many times we sin by being silent when we hear an untruth about people whom we don't particularly like.

Have you ever taken credit for something good that happened in the office or at home—and the credit was not rightfully yours? Later, when it is revealed that someone else should get all or most of the credit for the good outcome, you pretend not to hear it or try to explain it away with inadequate reasoning.

The end of Revelation 21:8 states, ". . . and all liars, their part will be in the lake that burns with fire and brimstone, which is the second death." Whenever we tell a little white lie, we are siding with Satan, the father of lies.

The temptation to exaggerate facts or circumstances is a constant battle for many people who are trying to be good Christians. It is so easy to add a word or extra sentence of explanation to make us or the circumstance look better. When I am caught in trying to explain an exaggerated statement, I find myself having to bend the truth to fit my statement. I always feel bad knowing I have not allowed God to use the "real happenings of the circumstance," rather than my overemphasis to bring attention to myself.

10. You Shall Not Covet

I always assumed this commandment meant not to be greedy or materialistic. Does this mean that I should not look upon my neighbor's new riding lawn mower with envy as I push my lawn mower in high grass?

1 Timothy 6:6-9 tells us, "But godliness actually is a means of great gain when accompanied by contentment. For we have brought nothing into the world, so we cannot take anything out of it either. If we have food and covering, with these we shall be content. But those who want to get rich fall into temptation and a snare and many foolish and harmful desires which plunge men into ruin and destruction."

Verse 17 says, "Instruct those who are rich in this present world not to be conceited or to fix their hope on the uncertainty of riches, but on God, who richly supplies us with all things to enjoy."

Before I was a Christian, I was looking for happiness. The media assured me if I bought the right car, wore the right clothes, or went on the right vacation, these things would bring me happiness. What I discovered was that I could not even define what the word "happiness" meant. Was I happy getting a good golf score? Or coaching the little league football team to victory? No, not really. I always wanted a lower golf score or for the team to make another touchdown.

After I accepted Christ, the Holy Spirit helped me see that money is to be used to serve both non-Christians and Christians. Money is not bad. It is the "love" of money that is the problem. Early in our Christian experience we all wanted to have more of the "good life," but we soon realized that contentment is really what we desired. This does not mean that we stop striving for excellence, but it does mean that we stop to smell the roses more often. We also thank God more often for what we have, rather than telling Him what we want. It is more fun to be excited and happy for a friend who has recently bought a new car or expensive coat than it is to covet their possessions.

The Bottom Line

James 2:10 tells us, "For whoever keeps the whole law and yet stumbles in one point, he has become guilty of all." Sin will separate us from God. Sin guilt will also result in our having fewer crowns to throw at the feet of Christ when we stand before Him on Judgment Day. Those of us who still think our self-righteous deeds will be "bartering-bait" with God will be disappointed. God has set the rules. We will be judged by God's rules—not what we think are the "fair" rules.

The Ten Commandments are wonderful tools to use with Muslims or Jews who feel Jesus is not the answer, but are well aware of the Ten Commandments. Following is a sample dialogue for talking with a Muslim:

"Bill, have you ever told a lie?" (Most will reply they have told a lie—at least a small, white lie.)

"Have you ever stolen anything?" (Most will reply they can remember stealing something in their past, but not recently.)

"Bill, the Bible says that if we males have looked upon a woman with lust in our heart, we are guilty of adultery." (Many men will reply that it is okay to "look if you do not touch.") I quickly remind them that that is man's interpretation of getting away with sin, rather than God's rule.

I then say, "So Bill, if you stood before God today, with your own admission, you would be a lying thief who has committed adultery. Is that correct?" (Many reply that if I take the Ten Commandments to their extreme, then they would be guilty.) "Therefore, Bill, you are guilty of three of the ten—and maybe all of the ten if we discussed them. What is your plan for asking God not to hold you accountable?"

Jews admit they no longer offer up animal sacrifices to wipe away their sin. Muslims admit they go to prayer four times a day to ask God to forgive their inadequacies. I explain, "Jesus Christ is the best solution I can find because He did it for me. I don't have to find a way to ask God to forgive me of my shortcomings, my inadequacies, my deceiving, my ego, my sin toward God. Christ did it for me. I did not do it for Him!"

Be sure to be very direct. If you know of certain sin patterns in a "good person," bring that area to his mind and let him know that God will take that sin seriously enough to separate him from Christ for eternity. Hell will be an awful place to spend eternity. A little confrontation on your part today can result in someone's happiness for eternity, as well as in that person's present walk on earth.

A good way to confront known sin patterns is to say, "How do you get rid of the guilt of your sin?" Listen to their answer and then say, "It appears to me that Christ is the easiest solution to the sin problem and removal of guilt."

You can use the illustration of a boy who told his mother how white their dog was against the green grass background. As winter came and the snow fell, he remarked that the dog did not seem so white against the snow. If you and I judge ourselves using the background of present everyday human standards, we come up clean. We can find plenty of people who are not as clean as we are. The average sinner looks fairly clean using this background of comparing one sin against another. God, however, will not judge us using everyday human standards but by the absolute standard of His Law. The Law is like pure white snow. Just like the dog, we are not a white color when compared to the snow. The point is "All have sinned and fall short" (Romans 3:23). Share with them that they need a Savior to help them become clean in God's eyes.

In the next chapter we will look at a particular set of Scriptures you can memorize and use—the time-tested "Romans Road to Salvation" which has brought many people into the Kingdom.

CHAPTER 12

Using the Romans Road to Salvation

"There is none righteous, not even one; there is none who understands, there is none who seeks for God"
(Romans 3:10-11).

There are many techniques you can use to share your faith in Christ. One popular and simple method is called the Romans Road. It's simple, because you use just a single book of the Bible—Romans—so you don't have to look for texts in a variety of books. Furthermore, the whole plan of salvation is clearly set forth in a compact series of verses in Romans.

Many people find that using Romans is an easy way to share their faith. By using the four selected scriptures in this one book, you can effortlessly take someone on a journey to accept Christ.

To use this technique, simply learn the location of the verses, open up your Bible, and read the verses. You have to memorize only Romans 3:23. In the margin of your Bible by verse 3:23 write 5:8;

that will be the second verse you use. Use the same procedure with 6:23 and 10:9-10.

Note the logical progression of these verses along the road:

Romans 3:23—"[F]or all have sinned and fall short of the glory of God." Explain that everyone since Adam and Eve, including you and the person you are witnessing to, has sinned. We are all guilty. That guilt bears a penalty.

Romans 5:8—"But God demonstrates His own love toward us, in that while we were yet sinners, Christ died for us." Christ died for my sins so I could have fellowship with Him as well as spend eternity in heaven with Him.

Romans 6:23—"For the wages of sin is death, but the free gift of God is eternal life in Christ Jesus our Lord." The penalty of sin is death, and separation from God is for eternity. God gave us a free gift, His Son, to pay those wages.

Romans 10:9-10—"… if you confess with your mouth Jesus as Lord, and believe in your heart that God raised Him from the dead, you shall be saved; for with the heart a man believes, resulting in righteousness, and with the mouth he confesses, resulting in salvation."

We all need to understand the facts of how Christ died on the cross for our sins, was resurrected in three days, and came back to earth to instruct the disciples. That knowledge results in righteousness. But in addition to that, we must also confess with our mouths our acceptance of those facts which will result in our salvation.

After having read and explained these verses from Romans, you can then proceed with the invitation, asking your friend if he or she is ready to pray the prayer of confession and accept Christ as Savior and Lord.

What can we learn from statistics? In the next chapter we look closely at the research findings of one of the top quantitative researchers in the area of religion and conversion. Knowing more of the context for our life and witness is important to our effectiveness.

CHAPTER 13

Statistics – Do They Matter?

This an exciting time to be alive for religious leaders who understand the spiritual search that millions of Americans have embarked upon and [who] are willing to engage with people who do not necessarily accept pat answers or traditional solutions to spiritual problems. Our society offers people a plethora of choices. Helping people to comprehend that spectrum of options and the consequences of their choices is one of the exciting challenges facing the religious leaders of our nation.

— George Barna, December 17, 2001

Barna must have had you and me in mind when he thought through the challenge to the Christian community!

In order to understand better what our neighbors are thinking, I have been compiling information from newsletters and books written by George Barna, president of the Barna Group. I have used italics to bring attention to information that applies to reaching others for Christ, and have placed in parenthesis my own comments on some of the items. I believe we can use these statistics to learn better how to start spiritual conversations with people who are lost.

For more information, go to the Barna website at *www.barna.org*. I know you will be blessed with learning what our relatives and friends are thinking, why they are thinking that way, why they are acting the way they do, and how to communicate with them more effectively.

What Faiths Are Represented in the US?

In his January 29, 2002 newsletter, Barna identifies five faith-based segments of the American population:

1. Evangelicals

This is a group of individuals who believe that their relationship with Jesus Christ will provide them with eternal life and who accept Bible teachings as accurate and authoritative. This group represents 15-20 million adults in the United States.

2. Non-Evangelical Born-Again Christians

This is a segment that also believes they have eternal salvation through the grace given them by God through their personal faith in Christ, but they do not believe in various core doctrines taught in the Bible. There are 65-70 million such adults in the United States.

3. Notional Christians

These people consider themselves to be Christians but do not claim they know their eternal destiny and have eternal life after death. They represent 90 million adults in the United States.

4. Atheistic or Agnostic

Atheists deny the existence of God while agnostics claim that you simply cannot know whether or not there is a god. Obviously both groups do not believe in God as Christians do. It is thought that there are 10-15 million such adults in the United States.

5. Other Faiths

Hindu, Muslim, Buddhism, etc. Combined, they represent 10-15 million adults in the United States. This breaks down to the following percentages:

- 8% of population—Evangelicals
- 33% of population—Non-evangelical, born-again Christians
- 44% of population—Notional Christians
- 8% of population—Atheist/Agnostic
- 7% of population—other faith groups.

The total born-again Christian population in the United States is currently approximately 41 percent of the total population.

Witnessing Opportunities

According to Barna, "In a typical week, 41 percent of the adults attending Christian churches are not born again." This means that there is a 40 percent chance that you and I may be sitting in church next to an individual who is playing a game with God and is not born again.

Barna suggests that "the nation seems mired in spiritual complacency." He notes that "Christian ministry is stuck in a deep rut and needs behavioral remodeling, strategic ministry, and a more urgent reliance upon God to change people's lives."

He points out, "Too many Christians and churches in America have traded in spiritual passion for empty rituals, clever methods, and mindless practices. The challenge of today's Church is not methodological. *It is a challenge to resuscitate the spiritual passion and fervor of the nation's Christians.*" Christians need to get excited about sharing their faith!

What Are Your Friends and Neighbors Thinking?

Barna tells us that 50 percent of adults want to find meaning and purpose in their lives. That means that about half of your neighbors would be willing to have an in-depth discussion concerning these issues.

"Fifty percent of adults say that they are still trying to find a few good friends." Seventy-five percent of those surveyed responded that they would "enjoy deep discussions with other people." Deep discussions certainly have to include questions such as, "What is truth?" and "Does God have a plan for my life?"

Barna found that four out of five people say their religious faith is very important in their life today. He notes, "*It would appear that a skeptical mind with a desire to learn more spiritual things is just exactly what you need to build a relationship with your next door neighbor.*"

It is interesting to note that 50 percent of the non-born again group said they are "deeply spiritual" and that 20 percent of them aligned themselves with the term "evangelical Christian." If half of the non-Christians say they are spiritual, why do we not think it is a fertile field for sharing our faith?

Amazing Finding

Barna says, "One of the most stunning outcomes was that born-again Christians and non-Christians were equally likely to be seeking meaning and purpose in life." It is hard to believe that fifty percent of the Christians were puzzled as to their purpose in life. Barna said:

> One of the primary values of the Christian faith is to settle the issue of meaning and purpose in life. The Bible endorses people's individual uniqueness but also provides a clear understanding of the meaning of life— that being to know love and serve God with all of your heart, mind, and strength. The widespread ignorance of that fundamental principle speaks volumes about the shallowness of America's faith—even among those who are most committed to faith matters.

If 50 percent of the Christians are still trying to find purpose and meaning in their lives, is it any wonder they are not excited or willing to share their faith in Jesus Christ—because it has not filled them?

The Unchurched

The Barna archives on unchurched people reveal these statistics:
- Seventy-five million adults in America are unchurched.
- Roughly ten million born-again Christians are unchurched.
- Men are one-third more likely than women to be

unchurched.

- 28% of married adults are unchurched.
- 54% of unchurched adults consider themselves Christians.
- 35% claim they have made a personal commitment to Jesus Christ that is still important in their life today.
- 65% say that Satan is not a living being but is a symbol of evil
- 57% believe that a good person can earn his or her way into Heaven.
- 51% assert that when Jesus Christ lived on earth, He committed sins.
- 23% firmly believe that the Bible is totally accurate in all that it teaches.

Goals and Priorities

Information in the archives on goals and priorities show these results:

- 91% of American adults list having good physical health as their top priority in life.
- 75% listed living with a high degree of integrity, having one marriage partner for life, having close friends, and having a clear purpose for living as top priorities of life.
- 70% say having a close, personal relationship with God is a top priority. (This means 70% of our neighbors/relatives want a relationship that is personal.)
- 53% identified being deeply committed to the Christian faith as a top priority.
- 42% said that being active in a local church is one of their top goals in life. (This means that four out of ten will go to church with you if you just ask them.)
- 71% of born again Christians list being active in a church as a top priority for their future.
- 53% of teens surveyed believe that the main purpose of life is enjoyment and personal fulfillment.

- 46% of teens surveyed indicated that it is more important to have a satisfying leisure life than a satisfying job or career.

Information on Witnessing

People often become Christians because of family influence. The following statistics from 1995 look at some of the more common ways people accept Christ. Even though this is an old statistic, I think it is still relevant to our witnessing efforts.

- conversation with family member—24%
- was raised by family to be a Christian—14%
- responded to a sermon at a church—14%
- conversation with a friend—10%
- was healed of a physical problem—6%
- attended an evangelistic event—5%
- relationship with a minister—5%
- death of a family member or friend—4%
- a Sunday school class or Bible study class—4%
- experience at a youth camp or youth event—4%
- watched an evangelistic TV program—3%
- read the Bible—3%
- birth of a child—2%

Barna has also shown in his updates some powerful statistics for reaching children when they are young:

- Children between ages 5 and 13 have a 32% probability of accepting Jesus Christ as their Savior.
- The probability of accepting Christ drops to 4% for those who are between the ages of 14 and 18.
- Those older than 18 have a 6% probability of accepting Jesus Christ as their Savior.

One very important element in witnessing has not yet been discussed. Prayer. Next, let's turn our attention to the need for prayer, and the ways in which God expects us to use prayer to prepare hearts.

CHAPTER 14

The Role of Prayer

A man who had been one of my instructors in dental school had a very large practice and referred dental implant patients to me. I came to know Bob fairly well. About ten years ago, while we were attending a dental meeting, Bob asked me "not to talk about God things" to his patients. His statement caught me off guard, and I did not reply. Two years later he asked me over the telephone to stop telling his patients about God. He informed me that he wanted his patients only to get dental implants, not a sermon. Four years later, Bob quit referring patients to me.

"May I Pray for You?"

Two years ago I saw Bob and his wife at a funeral. He was very kind. Wanda and I had gone to his daughter's wedding, and we talked about our children and how they had grown up. I noticed that he was breathing hard and inquired about his health. He informed me his asthma was getting worse and he was feeling tired. I said, "With your permission, may I put you on my prayer list?" He kindly accepted my offer.

Every month or two, I would call Bob and tell him I was praying, and ask how I could best pray for his needs. He would tell me, and

I would update my weekly prayer request for him. Of course, I also had his salvation as a weekly prayer request.

Some time later, Bob had a stomach infection and some heart problems. He was in the hospital in very serious condition. I called the hospital twice during his time in the cardiac intensive care unit and asked the receptionist to give him a message from Duke Heller. My message was, "Please tell Bob I am praying for him."

Prayer's Result

After Bob came home from the hospital, he was still very sick and missed some time at work. Fortunately, he had great partners who helped him. I called him a couple of times to ask how I could pray for him. I also talked with his wife once, asking how I could pray for him. Then I asked Bob if I could visit him, and he welcomed the request.

When I arrived, he was looking very tired. I used a lot of FORM questions to get a good background on the changes that had taken place in his life. He told me that he remembered having an out-of-body experience when he needed to have emergency care. His blood pressure dropped low and his heart rate was very high, which is a deadly combination. Just before he passed out, he felt as if he was above his body, watching as the doctors and staff shocked his heart and gave him medication to get his heart rate and blood pressure under control.

I asked him if he had felt his time on earth was over. He said that he honestly felt sure, at that exact moment in his life, that it was time for him to die.

Then I asked him, "Why do you think the Lord kept you alive?"

Bob replied, "I honestly believe the Lord has something else for me to do and that prayer kept me alive."

Wow! That was my opening to say, "Bob, I am sure the Lord kept you alive and that He has a special plan for your life. Can I ask you a question? If you had died and stood before God, and He had asked you why He should let you into heaven, what would you have said?"

"I would tell God that I have tried to do my best with my family and patients," Bob said.

"And if that is not enough?" I asked.

"I don't know what else would be needed," Bob said.

I asked him, "May I share something with you that someone once shared with me that made it easier for me to understand God?" I used the *Mayishare* brochure. Finally I reached the point where I asked the question, "Can you point to an exact time you accepted Christ as your Savior?"

Bob remained quiet for about a minute. Sixty seconds is a long period of silence! Then he admitted that he could not point to an exact time.

"Is there any reason you would not want to accept Christ now?" I asked him. He said there was no reason he could think of.

Bob prayed the prayer out loud to ask Christ to forgive him of his sins and become Lord of his life. We hugged each other as I left, and he walked me to the car. As we parted company, Bob grabbed my hand with both of his and said, "Thanks, Duke. That was special. I really appreciate your concern. Thanks for caring."

I looked at him and said, "You make a great day! Since you have Christ in your life now, you can really make it a great day.

His eyes glistening with tears, Bob told me, "I think I'm going to take a walk in the woods with God!"

As I backed my car out of his drive, I turned to wave goodbye, but Bob was walking with his head down into the woods behind his house. I knew that God had grabbed his heart.

God is so good! That day I learned an important lesson: Keep people on your prayer list for as many years as it takes.

The Example of Jesus

God answers prayer. Be a man or woman of prayer every day! Do what Jesus Christ did while He was on earth? He prayed! Luke 5:16

tells us, "[Jesus] Himself would often slip away to the wilderness and pray." Do we not think there was a reason Jesus spent the early hours of His day in prayer to the Father? He often rose before dawn to have unbroken fellowship with His Father (Mark 1:35). He also spent full nights in prayer (Luke 6:12).

Jesus was always submissive to the will of His Father. He found God's will by praying and asking directions for every task before Him. The secret to Christ's public ministry was His private ministry in prayer.

Prayer is the Christian's great secret weapon. Jesus told the disciples that ". . . they ought to pray and not to lose heart" (Luke 18:1). Paul instructs us to "pray without ceasing" (1 Thessalonians 5:17) and admonished Timothy, "First of all, then, I urge that entreaties and prayers, petitions and thanksgivings, be made on behalf of all men" (1 Timothy 2:1). James reminds us of the value of fervent prayer (James 5:16) and explains why sometimes our prayers are not answered, "You ask and do not receive, because you ask with wrong motives . . ." (James 4:3).

We learn in Luke 9:16-18 that Jesus blessed the food, giving thanks for its provision, before feeding the five thousand. Do you pray before each meal? In public? If the rest of the people sitting at your table start to eat their food, do you silently lower your head and pray, giving thanks for the food? If you are in a group of people you know fairly well, do you ask, "May I bless this food before we eat it?" I have never had anyone ask me not to pray for the food. I also cannot remember a time when, after the prayer, someone did not say, "Thank you. That was nice."

Do others see you praying? We should model Jesus' prayer habits in our lives. It is especially vital that our children observe our prayer life. Jesus taught others to pray through His example. Luke 11:1 states, "[I]t came about that while [Jesus] was praying in a certain place, after He had finished, one of His disciples said to Him, 'Lord, teach us to pray just as John also taught his disciples.'" This is one of the few requests the disciples made of Jesus. They observed Jesus praying, and after His prayer was finished, they asked Him to teach *them* how to pray properly. Obviously, the disciples had observed John the Baptist praying, as well. When they found Jesus on His knees, they observed Him in action.

What is Christ doing in heaven now? Do you suppose He is waiting for you and me to pray to Him? Every time you go to prayer, you are entering a prayer meeting with Jesus. He promised to be present where two or more are gathered. For what? To pray with you to the Father. He is using your own name. Jesus has the capability to pray for every prayer request we desire, but He cannot put our requests before His Father unless we make those requests known to Him through prayer.

Important Facts About Jesus and Prayer

- Christ, who lived on earth, prayed (Luke 6:12).
- Christ, who lives in heaven now, prays (Hebrews, 7:25).
- Christ and God the Father want you to pray (Matthew 6:6).
- Every time you pray, Christ is in prayer with you.
- In a mentoring relationship with His disciples, Christ taught them how to pray (Matthew 6:9-13).
- If Christ lives in you, He is going to develop in you a life of prayer (Colossians 4:2).

Why Do We Overlook Prayer in Our Private Lives?

The Christian at prayer stands between God and the devil, playing a vital role between heaven and hell. Ephesians 6:12 says, "For our struggle is not against flesh and blood, but against the rulers, against the powers, against the world forces of this darkness, against the spiritual forces of wickedness in the heavenly places."

As a praying Christian, you have no personal power or authority against Satan, but authority is delegated to you through Christ. He was victorious on the cross and we are united with Him by faith. Jesus was more concerned about the forces of evil that caused people to sin than wicked people who performed those sins.

Satan does not mind if you study the Word of God three hours a day, so long as you do not pray, because without prayer the knowledge will not become a part of your life. Satan does not mind if you share your faith if you do not pray, because it is easier to talk to men about God than it is to talk to God about men. Satan does not mind if you become very active in leadership of your local church if you do not pray, because you will not be able to accomplish anything significant for the Kingdom without prayer.

It is one thing to believe we have prayer power over Satan, but another thing to practice it. It is easier to pray for food or "things" than to pray for the stubbornness of our human hearts. It is not prayer that moves people, but the God to whom we pray.

Martin Luther had a plan for his day's work: "Work, work from early till late. In fact, I have so much to do today that I shall spend the first three hours in prayer."

Your *attitude* in how you share with others is also a crucial element in your witness. God cares about what your effective witness, of course, and He also cares about the affective. So let's discuss attitude a bit.

CHAPTER 15

Your Attitude—Positive is Better

Words can never adequately convey the incredible impact of our attitude toward life. The longer I live, the more convinced I become that life is 10 percent what happens to us and 90 percent how we respond to it.

I believe the single most significant decision I make on a day-to-day basis is my choice of attitude. It is more important than my past, my education, my bankroll, my successes or failures, fame or pain, what other people think of me or say about me, my circumstances, or my position. Attitude keeps me going or cripples my progress. It alone fuels my fire or assaults my hope. When my attitudes are right, there's no barrier too high, no valley too deep, no dream too extreme, no challenge too great for me.[1]

– Charles Swindoll

And so it is with us. We are in charge of our attitudes. Our attitude can attract more people to us than our Bible knowledge or our ability to quote Scripture. People like to be around cheerful,

---

[1] Charles R. Swindoll. *Strengthening Your Grip.* Nashville (W. Publishing Group, 1982) 206-207.

positive people. Positive Christians attract people to themselves. Christians who are negative thinkers about life's circumstances usually are unhappy. If we are unhappy with our circumstances most of the time, we will have difficulty sharing Christ. Others will not want to hear our opinions about spiritual things. We need to work hard to maintain a positive outlook at home, at work, and at church. Why would we *not* want to enjoy life to its fullest and live a positive, attractive life?

The Importance of Enthusiasm

Enthusiasm is one of the most powerful engines of success. When you do a thing, do it with all your might. Put your whole soul into it. Stamp it with your own personality. Be active; be energetic. Be enthusiastic and faithful and you will accomplish your objective. In the words of Ralph Waldo Emerson, "Nothing great was ever achieved without enthusiasm" ("Circles," *First Essays,* 1841).

How to Have a Positive Attitude

Let Your Light Shine.

If you are excited about being a Christian, tell your face. Smile a lot. Show your teeth. Grin and have fun—even in undesirable circumstances. Force yourself to be positive with everyone in your sphere of influence.

Maintain a clean appearance. Brush and floss your teeth so you will have clean breath while sharing the Gospel.

Judge Others with Kindness.

We usually judge ourselves by our *ideals* and others by their *actions*. When the other person gets mad, he is out of control. When we are angry, it is righteous indignation. When someone does not like one of our friends, he is prejudiced. When we do not like his friends, we are simply showing good judgment. When others take time to do things, they are slow. When we take extra time, we are being deliberate.

Offer others the same understanding of their motives that you want for yourself. When I truly care about people and sincerely try to help them achieve what they want in life, my life becomes much richer for doing it. As my attitude changes positively, I begin to attract people who are positive instead of people who are negative.

Remember to Express Gratitude.

Jesus once healed ten lepers. Only one returned to express gratitude. If you help people, let virtue be its own reward. Do it for the satisfaction of lending a hand, but don't expect them to be grateful. If someone has helped you by being a good friend, thank him at least twice for the deed. After every surgery procedure I perform, I thank the surgical assistants for their help. Without surgical assistants, most doctors would have low success rates of healing, because the patients would be in the operating room a very long time to accomplish a simple procedure.

While teaching doctors about staff relationships, I point out that I serve my staff. I serve them by thanking all of them before they leave the office at the end of the day. If by some chance I am still working at my desk when they are leaving for the day, they always stop to say good-bye and to get their well-deserved "thank you." I serve my staff by getting them a cup of coffee on occasions. I take pictures of their children playing soccer and give them the photographs as a keepsake. I ask about their family members and how I can pray for them.

How much of your prayer time is spent asking and how much is spent thanking God? It is not that God needs our gratitude, but we reveal our true selves when we only ask and don't say "thank you." Thank God for the people you work with and for your relatives, individually.

Learn to Accept Criticism without Taking Offense.

Constructive criticism is the building block to success—if we accept it for what it is, rather than try to defend our reasoning or actions. Unwanted criticism is usually helpful if we truly understand the meaning behind the criticism. If you have a mentor in your life, take the time to share with that person the criticism you have received, and get his or her reaction. Most of the time there is a great lesson God is going to teach us through that criticism.

Does criticism offend you unduly? Are you upset when you are maligned or someone misquotes you? Jesus was betrayed by one of His disciples, denied by another, doubted by a third, and misunderstood by all the others. He was despised and rejected for what He represented. If all this could happen to Jesus, there is no particular reason why we should expect to be free of criticism and rejection. (See John 15:18-20.)

Isn't it interesting that most presidents of the United States feel great if they get an approval rating of fifty to sixty percent? Every president knows that four out of ten people in our country don't like him and criticize him regularly.

The only way you and I can avoid criticism is to slip into the shadows of life, express no opinions, and do our best to be ignored. However, it is hard to witness if we are not involved in people's lives. If you are involved in people's lives, you will be criticized. Expect it!

Focus on the Needs of Others.

Life is full of trials. People need us to understand their problems so we can attempt to help in their present or future conflicts. The people you associate with are in one of three situations:

- A problem is about to come upon them.
- They are in the middle of a problem.
- They just got over a problem.

Remember that to feel significant is a fundamental human need. We help others feel significant by focusing on their needs.

Be Thankful for Your Job—or Get a New One.

It is hard to attract people to you if you are constantly complaining about your job and its problems. As a matter of a fact, you should be thankful for the troubles of your job. Those troubles provide most of your income, because if it were not for the things that go wrong, the difficult people you have to deal with, and the problems and unpleasantness of your working day, someone else could handle your job for half of what you earn.

It takes resourcefulness, patience, tact, knowledge, and courage to meet the troubles of most business days. If we would start to look for more troubles, learn to handle them with a smile, and see them as opportunities rather than irritations, we would find our lives are exciting because we have found significance in our jobs. Many big jobs are waiting for men and women who aren't afraid of the troubles connected with them.

Learn to Handle Interruptions Creatively.

During a hard day at work interruptions that seem unnecessary are difficult to handle. You find yourself asking, "Why can't people think for themselves?" "Why can't they just do it without asking for my advice?" Your time is limited and you have deadlines to meet. When people intrude on your time, you grow tense, then irritated, and finally exasperated.

Have you ever stopped to consider that the very frequency of your interruptions may be an indication of your value as a person? The people who are interrupted most often are those whose life and work are significant to others. Remember that every interruption is another opportunity to build a bridge to that individual.

Most of us need patience to handle interruptions from our small children, especially after a full day of interruptions at work. Children need to feel significant, especially to their parents. Have you ever noticed that if your child is going to dive off a diving board, he always calls out your name and asks you to watch him? Allow your children to interrupt you now so that they will want to spend time with you in the future when you are interrupting their schedule.

Interruptions require us to listen, *really listen*, to our spouse, our children, and our colleagues. A genuine listener seeks to understand another without prejudgment. Don't give the answer before you have heard the problem completely stated. Someone once said, "A problem is often half-solved when it is stated." My wife, Wanda, is constantly reminding me, "Be there when you are there."

I take interruptions as coming from the Lord. They belong in my schedule, because my schedule is God's to arrange at His pleasure. If a Christian comes to me and my schedule is full, I will say, "The Lord must have brought you here. Let us pray and find out why He sent you. I know you are busy, so we can save time if we find out how God thinks I can be of help."

Interruptions can drain your energy. The world is run by tired men and women. Fatigue is the price paid to serve the Lord. Mediocrity is the result of never getting tired. It is okay to be tired. Even Jesus grew weary in His ministry and had to rest (John 4:6). Christians know where to find renewal. Second Corinthians 4:16 reminds us, "Therefore we do not lose heart…"

"Pay Ahead."

Former Ohio State University football coach Woody Hayes always taught his assistant coaches to "pay ahead." This involves helping people without any thought of reward or benefit. If you do, the reward will follow, maybe not as you thought, but it will come to you. He was not saying to plan a nice act, hoping that you would benefit. Instead, help people with kindness as your only motive.

Coach Hayes used to visit hospitalized athletes, many of them not even football players. He would tell them that he wanted to brighten up their day, and he hoped they would get better and be able to compete in their sport. His acts of kindness brought many great young athletes to Ohio State, even though that was not his original reason for visiting them.

I discovered at an early age that most of the differences between average people and people of achievement can be explained with two words: "extra effort." Quality people who achieve do what is expected of them, and then some. They can be counted on in an emergency situation.

Think of those times when you made an effort that was difficult or more than expected. Wasn't there a great feeling of accomplishment? That same feeling is available if you go out of your way to "pay ahead" in helping others without being asked.

Learn to Accept Yourself—and Love Yourself.

Self-love is not the same as egotism. You are to love yourself as you love your neighbor. Not only are you entitled to love yourself, you are expected to do so. You can love another person only to the degree that you love yourself.

God made us with our personality, temperament, and limitations. We all need to improve in most areas of our lives, but we must also accept who we are in Christ. I am a high-energy person who has had the pleasure of working hard and seeing the fruits of that labor. Why would I want to change who I am—who God made me to be?

Your personality is the exact personality that God is going to use to reach others. Don't try to be someone else when you share Christ. Use your personality and realize that God has made you special.

Allow a Lot of Humor in Your Life.

Learn to stand outside yourself and your circumstances, see things in perspective, and then laugh. It is a great safety valve. You will never lead others far without the joy of the Lord and a sense of humor. Life really is full of joy--and funny! Humor with a loud belly laugh makes the worst of circumstances seem less difficult.

Our sense of humor is a gift from God that should be controlled and cultivated. Clean, wholesome humor will relax tension and relieve difficult situations. A good test of the appropriateness of a joke is whether the humor controls us or we control it. Know the place for a clean joke and try to use it to illustrate a spiritual truth if possible.

Discipline Yourself

Sometimes you will become discouraged and lose heart. Some days you will not want to get out of bed to fight the battle again. That is when character and commitment need to take over. Character will get us out of bed. Commitment will move us into action, and discipline will enable us to follow through with what we need to do. Without the essential quality of discipline, all other God-given gifts cannot grow to maturity. *Discipline is probably the most important virtue we possess.*

Many who aspire to leadership fail because they have never learned to follow. We must learn to obey a discipline imposed from without and then take on a more rigorous discipline from within. Those who rebel against authority and refuse self-discipline are not qualified to lead others—in our homes or in our offices. Lazy and disorganized people never rise to God's desire for their lives. Many people are sufficiently gifted but have large areas of life floating free from the Holy Spirit's control.

Procrastination is the number one enemy to self-discipline. It causes more heartache, more stress, and more failure in business and ministry than anything else I can imagine. Learn to dispatch the hardest tasks first and then go to the easier items. Prioritizing is a learned skill and can be used to help us achieve all that God intended us to accomplish.

> God, harden me against myself,
> The coward with pathetic voice
> Who craves for ease and rest and joy.
> Myself, arch-traitor to myself,
> My hollowest friend,
> My deadliest foe,
> My clog, whatever road I go.
> — J. Oswald Sanders, *Spiritual Leadership*
> (Chicago: Moody Press), page 53

Force Yourself to Write Thank-You Notes.

A great way to get the opportunity to witness is by saying "thank you." When was the last time you got a thank-you note from someone? Did you enjoy it? Of course you did. I have sent thank-you notes to referring doctors or patients for years. In fact, I developed a "thank-u-gram" with a tooth logo on the envelope. I built a tremendous practice by seeking out someone every day who had helped me and sending him or her a thank-u-gram. Can you imagine the look on the face of the gas-station attendant who gets a thank-u-gram from someone because he helped him put air in his tires?

Thank-u-grams are different from letter writing. They just tell someone he or she brightened your day by being part of it. Many people are in the Kingdom today because of a thank-you note, sent immediately after an event that showed a thankful heart for a deed well done. Our staff sends one of these dental thank-u-grams to a selected "patient of the day." This kindness has led to many opportunities to share Christ with patients. Some patients have shown me thank-u-grams they have carried in their purse or wallet for years. A properly directed thank-you note can touch the heart of a seeker.

Overcome Your Fear for Christ's Sake and for Your Relatives' Sakes.

Philippians 4:13 says, "I can do all things through Him who strengthens me." Romans 8:31 tells us, "If God is for us, who is against us?" First John 4:4 affirms, ". . . greater is He who is in you than he who is in the world."

Forget about past rejections and failures you have experienced in witnessing. All of those past events are now non-issues. Your friends and relatives need to be reached with the Gospel, and you are the one God can use to reach them.

Often when I do what the Lord is directing me to do, I am petrified, but I care enough for the cause or the person that I will ignore that funny feeling in my stomach—and just do it! Second

Corinthians 12:10 says, "Therefore I am well content with weaknesses, with insults, with distresses, with persecutions, with difficulties, for Christ's sake; for when I am weak, then I am strong."

Remember that courage is being afraid, but doing it anyway. Let compassion for the people who matter swallow your fears, and let the fear of the Lord be your servant. Psalm 118:6 reminds us, "The Lord is for me; I will not fear; what can man do to me?" John Wesley said, "Get on fire for God and people will come to watch you burn!" Remember, there are only two times we should preach the Word: "In season and out of season" (2 Timothy 4:2).

God's will is for all men to be saved and come to a knowledge of truth as stated in 1 Timothy 2:3-4: "This is good and acceptable in the sight of God our Savior, who desires all men to be saved and to come to the knowledge of the truth." Your relatives and friends fall under the category of "all men."

From presidents to stock clerks, we are all on a mission. However, it is not our mission; it is God's mission. That is why you were brought into this world at this specific time. It is not because you have something great to bring to the table. God wants to show the world, including your relatives and friends, what He can do through you. Remember where you are and what you are about, and you are never going to become stale in your journey with God. Bob Burney, a local Christian radio host, always closes his shows with this statement: "Remember whose you are!"

A relationship with Jesus is not about escape. It is a call to engagement. Jesus invited Peter to step out of the boat. He summoned Zacchaeus to get out of the tree and become the person God created him to be. He called Lazarus out of his grave.

Success always involves risk—if you are going to get to second base, you must get your foot off first base. Martin Luther said, "The fruit of the Gospel, that which God expects from man can grow only from the soil of obedience. In this process, man no longer needs to consider what he is to achieve. Freed from the anxiety of failure, he is capable of the highest endeavor because the source of his capacity to bear fruit lies outside himself, the yield is certain. It counts and abides for eternal life."

Remember, you will take only two things to heaven: God's Word and the people you and the Holy Spirit worked together to bring there. You will not take your bank account, your favorite putter, or a letter from a loved one. The only thing you can take into heaven is eternal fruit—the lives of those in whom you planted seed and allowed the harvest to be reaped.

Pastor Lee Ault once said in a sermon, "An interesting thing about fruit in the natural is that a man can prepare for and encourage the growth of fruit but he can expect and receive it only as a gift. The seed and harvest are bestowed upon him. To what extent the growth of the fruit is removed from human will power is shown by the fact it ripens at its appointed time. Man cannot determine the time of ripening of fruit."

The seed you and I plant in the lives of others determines the form of fruit that will ripen. We have to plant *Jesus*; the Holy Spirit will cause the fruit to grow and ripen into God's fruit that will include your relatives, neighbors, and friends.

We next turn to a fascinating topic—what are people thinking as they hear the Gospel for the first time? For a look inside the minds of some who have made commitments to Christ, read on!

CHAPTER 16

What Are They Really Thinking?

Over the years, I have had many opportunities to use the *Mayishare* brochure or the Bridge illustration to help people find Christ. You might well ask, "Does sharing your faith really produce lasting results?" I've wanted to know, also, how long-lasting and positive the results of my witnessing might have been.

So, in an effort to find out what converts were thinking that helped them come to Christ, I sent surveys to a large number of them, asking about the circumstances of their commitment and about the effectiveness of the *Mayishare* brochure. The responses were encouraging, and I share some of them here.

Changed Lives

"I Understood for the First Time"

I attended a class at my church called "May I Share Something with You?" based on the brochure and taught by Duke Heller. Ironically, I attended the class with the expectation of being able to share my faith with others. I didn't know until we started going through the brochure that I had absolutely no knowledge of the things contained inside. I had never heard the explanation of the relationship between me, a sinner, Jesus Christ, and God put in this context before. It had an enormous and life-changing impact on me. I asked Duke to stay around after the class for a minute and began crying while trying to tell him that I understood for the first time in my life. I truly got it!

I cried and cried as the truth of what Jesus had done for me sank in—and I felt an enormous wave of relief that I had started down the path He wanted me to follow. As I sat there with Duke, I felt like the moon, the stars, the planets, and all the weight of my life had been lifted off my shoulders. I handed it all over to God right then.

I knew right away that I wanted Jesus to be in charge of my life. I asked Duke to wait after class so I could tell him what had happened to me. I don't think I made much sense at first because I was trying to tell him what a profound impact this had on me but between the sobs of joy, it was probably very difficult to understand exactly what I was saying. But it didn't matter; I knew that I finally had found the answer to my questions.

Don't be surprised if you change someone's life right there on the spot. But don't be discouraged if you don't see it happen. This is a powerful brochure. Jesus will do the work. Use this to start the conversation, but don't expect results and most of all don't lose your enthusiasm if nothing seems to come of it. You may not know, they may not tell you, but Jesus knows. Sow the seed—as many times as you can with whomever you can.

Duke didn't know that Jesus really had entered my heart that night. I imagine that he's been used by Jesus many more times than he knows. God brought him back into my life so I could tell him just how much he helped me.

My husband and I were dedicating our children at church and the night before, the phone rang. It was Duke Heller, introducing himself and his wife as our prayer partners during the service. He had no idea who I was, but I sure knew who he was! I remember saying something like, 'Duke! You brought me to Jesus! I attended your class!' He said, 'I did?' and I went into the whole story of the class, the brochure—kept him on the phone for a long time. I couldn't believe that of all the people who could have prayed with us for our kids' dedication, Duke was the one calling me!

I no longer believe in coincidence. Later on, I e-mailed Duke and told him how important he was to me. I found out through e-mailing a couple of times that Duke was considering not doing the May I Share class any more. I remember writing to him asking him to reconsider because if there was only one person who showed up for that class, it could be another person like me—someone who thinks he or she knows what the truth is and flat-out doesn't.

What Is Success?

My wife and I had met with Duke and Wanda concerning success in business. Duke indicated that to have success, a person first needed to have a relationship with Jesus. He said, "Here's how it works...." I did not accept Christ that night.

In the fall of 1990 my twin sons were in the hospital after having been born three months prematurely. One of them almost died while I was visiting him at the hospital. This was the second such occurrence, and I was at his cribside for both occasions. After the second time, I was searching for answers, comfort, and guidance. I went home, pulled my Bible off the shelf and started reading and studying. In my Bible I found the Bridge diagram that Duke had shown me on his family room couch probably six months before. Now I was ready. I followed Duke's written instruction, studied the verses he had suggested, and asked Jesus into my life.

More Testimonies

I accepted Christ on a Tuesday morning as I was driving to work. Duke had just shown me a hand-drawn version of the *Mayishare* brochure that morning over breakfast. I was interested in and had been seeking/praying for a definitive way to understand and relate to God. I think it was especially important that the reasoning started in Genesis with the fall of man. That was the hook for me that made it easy to understand why Christ had to die for man. I was asked how I hoped to get to heaven. Then my idea was compared to the Bible. I just knew the Bible was right.

A colleague shared that he first was exposed to the Bridge concept at a dental seminar.

A few of us met Duke by the pool on a Sunday morning, and he shared the Lord with us for an hour. I didn't understand it at first, but I knew God was speaking to me. It motivated me to search for the answer. A year later I found a church that has become my family. Five years after that, I finally understood what it meant to be re-born, and gave my life to Christ.

Another response illustrates the importance of asking the right questions.

I met with Duke at his office. We were initially discussing business. The conversation turned to personal issues (I was struggling with many at the time) and then to my relationship with Christ. I knew that Duke and Wanda had a peace that I was looking for. I grew up going to Sunday school, church, youth group, etc., but no one had ever asked me if I had accepted Jesus Christ as my personal Savior. This was the first time anyone asked me to make a commitment to Christ, and I did it right then.

Sometimes people need a very direct approach. Don't ever give up, and don't be afraid to confront. This is illustrated by one individual.

Duke had been talking with me for at least six months before my heart softened to receive God's gift of eternal life. Duke actually had to confront me, sternly, and point out that I had to choose: 'Stand with Him or against Him.' So, I received this great gift of my salvation and now stand with Christ.

"Don't give up—you are not going to save everyone. Remember, even Jesus did not convert everyone. But always keep trying."

I think many people will accept Jesus when they're alone. I like the *Mayishare* brochure because it gives people something by which to remember our conversation, and it gives them something to go through step-by-step to ask Jesus into their life. I think the brochure is powerful, too, in the fact that as a sharer of Christ, I've got an outline of the conversation I want to have with that person. I can end the conversation and leave the person knowing that I have covered the points necessary. The rest is up to [him or her].

I think that a lot of people who don't know the Lord, especially younger folks, don't realize their need for a savior. They don't think of themselves as sinners—most see themselves as 'a good person.' They also don't understand the holiness of God and how He abhors sin. Without this knowledge, they have trouble seeing the 'good news' of the Gospel. I think people who are in hard times in their life because of bad decisions are more open to hearing the Gospel.

Duke showed me the brochure at his office after a business meeting. God used the brochure to soften my heart so that when I went to a Bill Gothard seminar I was ready to make a decision for Christ. The brochure raised practical questions in my mind about what this present life is all about and what would happen to me when I died. It showed me there was a way to know for sure where I would spend eternity.

Survey Responses

A section of the survey said, Describe your feelings as you came to realize the importance of making a personal commitment to the Lord. Here are a few comments as people wrote them:

"Peace, wonder, what to do next, who to talk to, excitement, you name it!"

"Peace, pressure off me, a feeling of life and love."

"I felt unworthy and unclean. Because of my upbringing in my family's religion, I thought I had to clean myself up before accepting God's grace. But Duke explained I didn't need to do this, using Scripture to show me the truth."

"Peace, excitement, warmth. Guilt, shame and sadness for Christ's suffering. Guilt and shame for years of neglecting my original commitment."

"I had a feeling of excitement and wanted to share that with everyone I loved (family, friends, and fellow workers)."

"I felt a sense of responsibility, commitment and trust that the Lord will support and guide me through life if I just allow Him to through worship and communication."

"Excited. I wondered also why it had taken me so long to come to Him."

"I was relieved to know that I no longer needed to wonder whether heaven was an option for me. I also remember being concerned about the salvation of my children."

"I felt peaceful, happy, and a sense of understanding and purpose for what I was seeking came over me."

"Relaxed, excited, warm, and I thought of all the different things my grandmother had taught me."

"It felt awkward for me to pray to receive Christ in the middle of a restaurant, but I realized that the information given to me was an answer to my prayers. I didn't feel any different, but in a few days I became aware that my thinking was changing."

"A great load was lifted from my shoulders."

The last question on the survey was, "Is there any other information you would like to share about the *Mayishare* brochure and its use and effectiveness?" Here are a few of the responses to that question:

"The bridge hit home for me, and I feel it is an intellectual and uplifting way to explain what is missing in our lives and what we can do to fix the 'vacuum' in our lives."

"It takes the pressure off the one presenting to be the answer man or the know-it-all. It's non-confrontational."

"Many people receive information best in a visual form; the Bridge provides that needed picture for them. The brochure or drawing allows you both to focus on something together, as opposed to your being in a position of talking *at* the person you are sharing with and causing the person to be on the defensive."

"Be careful to pick the right circumstances. I know you have to take a chance, but be careful not to turn someone off to the Word. Let them see it working in your life before you share the brochure."

"I truly appreciate the character and graphic demonstration to help me reaffirm my dormant but steadfast love for life and Christ. It is hard for me to share with others knowing of possible rejection. In time and with confidence things become easier."

"Keep it simple. What Duke shared with me was simple and direct. It made sense. I could understand it. It gave me hope. It began a transformation that continues."

Those are just a few of the responses from people who have been "on the other side of the fence." It's encouraging to see the many ways God works in hearts to draw people to Himself. I pray that these responses will be a challenge to you to step out into your world and share with others your faith in Christ.

Being courageous for God sometimes brings on us persecution or harassment. In our final chapter, we'll discuss how to handle opposition that may come.

CHAPTER 17

No Matter What

"I would rather fail in a cause that will ultimately succeed than succeed in a cause that will ultimately fail."

(Pat Morley. The Man in the Mirror. Grand Rapids: Zondervan)

Opposition to Witnessing

At some point, you will probably receive some kind of harassment for your faith. When facing such a situation, it's important to keep your perspective. Your question should be, "What does Christ desire for me?"

Paul tells us in Galatians 2:20: "I have been crucified with Christ; and it is no longer I who live, but Christ lives in me; and the life which I now live in the flesh I live by faith in the Son of God, who loved me, and delivered Himself up for me." Christ lives in you and in me. We have been crucified *with* Christ. We must handle challenges and suffering as He did.

Paul also tells us in Philippians 1:21: "For to me, to live is Christ, and to die is gain." Why would Paul say this? He knew that when he died he would get more of Christ. Even if we have to die for His sake, it is gain.

Marlene Bagnull, a friend who helped edit this book, reminded me of an old story about a frog. The frog was put in a pan of room temperature water on the stove. The temperature was increased slowly, until the frog was boiled. Because the temperature increased gradually, the frog did not realize it was in danger until it was too late to escape. Marlene reminded me that our society is like the frog. Our culture is slowly boiling us, and we don't notice how it affects us. Our freedom to witness as we have in the past could gradually be taken away before we even realize it.

Who knows how much longer we will enjoy the freedom we now have to share our faith? Will we always be able to read a book on evangelism without fear of persecution? Will we always be able to place messages in the newspaper about the outreach activities of our churches? How much longer will it be legal in the United States to hand out tracts on the streets or at a crowded football game?

Certain political activists are constantly looking for ways to change the laws to inhibit our freedom of choice or expression, since it may cause someone mental distress. We must realize there is urgency to share our faith now, because tomorrow our freedom to do so may be taken away.

Rejected By Loved Ones

One of the hardest things to deal with is rejection by our own relatives or close friends because of our faith. I am reminded of the time two brothers came to me asking if I would do the "bridge evangelism presentation" for their parents. The father and I had been friends since dental school. He was retired from teaching at the dental school. His son had played baseball on one of my teams. He was a very kind and gentle man. He and his wife were truly two of the nicest people I have ever known. They would be on your list of "good people." Both were entrenched in believing that "works" would be their ticket to heaven.

The sons came to me explaining they had gone to their parents and shared Christ with them. As a result, their parents were very upset. The mother was especially upset, as she felt she was doing fine in "her religion" and did not need their "new-found born-again religion."

I called them and asked if Wanda and I could come over to their house. I told Dick I wanted to tell him what I was going to do with the rest of my life. When we arrived, we spent some time talking about their sons and grandchildren. Then I asked if I could share what I was going to do with the rest of my life.

They were very gracious and allowed me to go through the *Mayishare* brochure until I got to the part, "Can you point to an exact time you accepted Christ?" At that point they informed me, "You are beginning to sound like our sons." The mother became visibly angry; the father became very quiet.

I explained that I was trying to show them how I was going to spend the rest of my life, but I realized they were not receptive to my presentation. Wanda and I thanked them for giving us their time and left. Wanda felt bad, but I felt great—God's Word is sharper than a two-edged sword.

Handling Harassment for your Faith

Here are a few things to remember when faced with harassment or misunderstanding for your faith. First, remember that Jesus said, "Blessed are those who have been persecuted for the sake of righteousness, for theirs is the kingdom of heaven. Blessed are you when men cast insults at you, and persecute you, and say all kinds of evil against you falsely, on account of Me. Rejoice, and be glad, for your reward in heaven is great, for so they persecuted the prophets who were before you" (Matthew 5:10-12).

The Reality of Harassment

We can expect harassment and persecution. Note that Jesus said "when people insult you."

The Reason for Harassment

We're talking about persecution for the sake of Christ, "on account of Me." Jesus told His disciples, "Remember the word that I said to you, 'A slave is not greater than his master,' If they persecuted Me, they will also persecute you" (John 15:20). The apostle Paul also pointed out, "And indeed, all who desire to live godly in Christ Jesus will be persecuted" (2 Timothy 3:12).

The Response to Harassment

"For our struggle is not against flesh and blood, but against the rulers, against the powers, against the world forces of this darkness, against the spiritual forces of wickedness in the heavenly places" (Ephesians 6:12).

Refuse to Retaliate

"Never pay back evil for evil to anyone. Respect what is right in the sight of all men" (Romans 12:17).

Respond Positively

"Do not be overcome by evil, but overcome evil with good" (Romans 12:21). "[L]ove your enemies, and pray for those who persecute you" (Matthew 5:44).

Reasons to Rejoice

It Means God's Spirit Can Be Seen in Your Life. "If you are reviled for the name of Christ, you are blessed, because the Spirit of glory and of God rests upon you" (1 Peter 4:14).

It Means God Can Trust You. "So they went on their way from the presence of the Council, rejoicing that they had been considered worthy to suffer shame for His name" (Acts 5:41).

It Is Temporary. "For momentary, light affliction is producing for us an eternal weight of glory far beyond all comparison" (2 Corinthians 4:17). These troubles won't last very long, yet this short time of distress will result in God's richest blessing upon us forever and ever.

Remember Your Reward for Sharing Your Faith

"[A]nd if children, heirs also, heirs of God and fellow-heirs with Christ, if indeed we suffer with Him in order that we may also be glorified with Him" (Romans 8:17). Since we are God's children—if we share Christ's suffering, we will also share in His glory.

Remain Faithful

"Therefore, let those also who suffer according to the will of God entrust their souls to a faithful Creator in doing what is right" (1 Peter 4:19).

A Personal Testimony

A friend of mine, Jim W., sent me an e-mail after he shared his faith with his family. He has given me permission to use it in this book because the experience freed him. I am copying his e-mail word for word, in order to keep the impact as you read it:

Dear Duke,

On Easter Sunday, after prayer and preparation, I was determined to share the gospel with my two younger brothers. They both know I left our former church, but there has never been any conversation on spiritual matters and the reason for our leaving.

Recently, my sister tried to explain to one brother why she left our former church. He went off on her like he went off on me Easter Sunday. He flat out refused to listen to a word I said and then told me he was offended that I would even think he would need any help understanding spiritual matters. He would not let me offer any response. He would ask questions and cut me off in every instance.

He finished by repeatedly yelling at me that I was brainwashed before walking into the house.

After a stunned moment of silence, my dad, who witnessed all of this conversation, said to me, "Well, I guess you've got to do what you've got to do." And then he walked away.

I say all of this not because I want sympathy from Christian friends. What happened is about what I expected and happens to Christians all the time. The truth is that the Holy Spirit has been pressing me to do this for a few years, but it never seemed like the right time. It was simply fear at work and not faith. It was disobedience. My perspective was warped—I cared more about what they thought of me than the glory it would bring to God.

Now, I have shared the good news with all of my immediate family. I will continue to ask God to help them see the light, but I no longer feel that particular burden. In fact, God has given me an extra measure of boldness. I would encourage anyone who is holding out on God and their family to forget their pride and find a way to get the job done. I needed help so I asked God to make a way for me to witness to my brothers and He did.

By the way, my youngest brother and his wife are looking for a new church and he was genuinely appreciative of the materials I brought for him.

Signed sincerely,
Jim W.

The apostle Paul said, "But having the same spirit of faith, according to what is written, 'I believed, therefore I spoke,' we also believe, therefore also we speak" (2 Corinthians 4:13). Paul spoke what he believed. Jim W. spoke what he believed. God honored Paul's boldness; He will also honor Jim's boldness.

Did the Holy Spirit just bring someone to your mind with whom you must have the boldness to go share *now*? You can know the joy that boldness brings to those who rely on the Holy Spirit to lay the groundwork for their witness. Remember, hell is for real and for eternity.

A Burning Fire

"But if I say, 'I will not remember Him or speak any more in His name,' then in my heart it becomes like a burning fire shut up in my bones; and I am weary of holding it in, and I cannot endure it" (Jeremiah 20:9). Jim W. had a burning fire inside of him that he could not keep shut up in his heart.

Another young friend of mine, Mark W., has a fire that is burning in him to share his faith with any who will listen. Mark is always telling me about people he is building bridges to and how the Lord is allowing him to be part of others accepting Christ. Is there a burning fire in your belly that you need to release to your relatives and friends?

I have had the distinct privilege to be involved in the life of a businessman, Joseph M., who was very successful financially before coming to Christ. Joseph lived in the Cleveland, Ohio, area and worked 90-100 hours a week building his dream—only to have his boss tell him late on New Year's Eve that he was going to have to let him go, even though he was one of the most successful people he had working for him at the time. (Can you imagine working late into the evening of New Years Eve?) Joseph's boss was going to take the company in a different direction, and Joseph was not part of that direction. After losing his job, Joseph committed his life to Christ. He then had a bout with cancer.

God put a burning in his belly to share the Gospel with people in the business world. He worked very hard for five years to learn a new job and be successful at that job. He was looked upon by his colleagues as a fierce competitor in the business world but also as someone who maintained good moral character. He refused to be alone with a woman. He also did not take part in "office gossip."

Joseph was asked to do something he felt was not morally correct. He explained to his boss that he could not do it. His boss informed him, "You will never be successful in our business unless you overlook small items like this."

My friend quit that position and studied for five months for a new career. He is now just starting a new profession that I feel certain God will bless. It is amazing when God puts a burning in our belly; it becomes part of our everyday lives, especially in the business world. I am really proud of Joseph.

He is not bashful about what Christ has done in his own life and daily stands on biblical principles in the workplace. Joseph knows that God will give him opportunities to witness in the business world if he keeps the burning in his belly for unsaved businessmen.

He recently called me, asking advice on how to witness to a friend who was sick in the hospital and perhaps dying. He used some of my suggested wording and had the great honor of leading the individual to a saving knowledge of Jesus Christ.

Joseph later told me, "It was one of the greatest feelings in my life, after he died, knowing that he was having supper with the Lord that night." God can change your workplace or home, your friends and loved ones, if you find a burning in your belly to share your faith.

Paul said in 2 Corinthians 9:6, "Now this I say to you, he who sows sparingly shall also reap sparingly; and he who sows bountifully shall also reap bountifully." God is willing and able to put a burning in our belly if we will sow bountifully, leaving the bountiful reaping to the Holy Spirit.

My Prayer for You as You Finish This Book

I would hope and pray that you will close your eyes *now* and think of your close relatives. These are the most important people in your life. List them by name and add their telephone numbers. Call them today or tomorrow to set up an appointment with the purpose of sharing Jesus Christ. Use whatever method you wish: your personal walk with Christ and how He has influenced your life, the Romans Road, or the *Mayishare* brochure.

You must pray each day for each person on your list. Pray that the Holy Spirit will prepare the hearts of your relatives or friends for your gospel presentation.

You did not read this book by accident. You read this book because the Holy Spirit wanted you to learn that you can share your faith with boldness.

I conclude with a note from the late Bill Bright, founder of Campus Crusade for Christ. It is certainly a challenge that Christians should heed today.

Imagine for a moment that you are an extremely zealous witness for Christ. You are sharing the message of God's great love and forgiveness where you go. You are able actually to lead ten people a day to our Savior. Using "spiritual addition," that would be 3,650 people per year!

That is an amazing number. Yet, at that rate it would take you thousands of years to reach the world! But thankfully, God has given to us a miraculous method, "spiritual multiplication," through which we can reach the world in our generation. Spiritual multiplication is the deliberate discipling of new Christians so that they in turn will evangelize and disciple others.

Using this technique, instead of leading 3,650 people a year to Christ, you lead only ten people, then disciple them to witness to and disciple ten others. Each of the new believers, now a 100, can in turn do the same for ten more, which would then be 1,000, and on and on. By this multiplication strategy, you could theoretically reach the entire world of more than six billion people in less than ten years!

- from INSIGHTS from Bill Bright,
Campus Crusade for Christ

Wow, what a challenge! May we be faithful, not only in evangelizing but in discipling!

I would like to hear your story of how God used this material in your life. Please send me a note to the following address or personally call me at home to discuss your successes. May God continue to bless you richly as you trust Him day after day after day!

Make a great day for Christ *today!*

Dr. Alfred "Duke" Heller
6586 Worthington-Galena Road
Worthington, Ohio 43085
Home ~ 614-888-4830
Fax ~ 614-885-9314
E-mail ~ *dukeheller@copper.net*
yes@mayishare.com

Cut-Out Card

You may find it helpful to carry these "Top Five Questions" in your pocket, wallet or purse to assist in your witness for Christ. We suggest you photocopy this card, enlarging or reducing as necessary, and then laminate it against wear and tear as you carry and use it.

How to Start a *Kingdom* CONVERSATION

TOP FIVE QUESTIONS

1. With your permission, may I pray for your situation?
2. Do you believe God answers prayer?
3. What do you think about God?
4. Who do you think Jesus Christ was?
5. May I share something with you that someone shared with me that made it easier for me to understand God?

How to Start a *Kingdom* CONVERSATION

TOP FIVE QUESTIONS

1. With your permission, may I pray for your situation?
2. Do you believe God answers prayer?
3. What do you think about God?
4. Who do you think Jesus Christ was?
5. May I share something with you that someone shared with me that made it easier for me to understand God?